Broadway Christian Church Fort Wayne
Cleaning Up the Clutter
Barnes, Emilie   CL14 Bar

0000 6194

P9-EMH-214

Cleaning Up *the* Clutter

Emilie Barnes

HARVEST HOUSE PUBLISHERS

EUGENE, OREGON

Verses marked NIV are taken from the HOLY BIBLE, NEW INTERNATIONAL VERSION®. NIV®. Copyright © 1973, 1978, 1984 by the International Bible Society. Used by permission of Zondervan. All rights reserved.

Cover by Terry Dugan Design, Minneapolis, Minnesota

Cover photo © Victoria Pearson/Taxi/Getty Images

CLEANING UP THE CLUTTER
Formerly titled Simply Organized

Copyright © 1998 by Harvest House Publishers
Eugene, Oregon 97402
www.harvesthousepublishers.com

Library of Congress Cataloging-in-Publication Data

Barnes, Emilie.
    Cleaning up the clutter / Emilie Barnes.
        p. cm.
    ISBN 0-7369-0979-6 (pbk.)
    1. Housekeeping. 2. House cleaning. I. Title.
TX301.B27 2004
640—dc22   2003020995

All rights reserved. No part of this publication may be reproduced, stored in a retrieval system, or transmitted in any form or by any means—electronic, mechanical, digital, photocopy, recording, or any other—except for brief quotations in printed reviews, without the prior permission of the publisher.

Printed in the United States of America

05 06 07 08 09 10 11 / BP-MS / 10

Contents

Me, Get Organized?

Over the years I have received countless letters from women who want to know how to get organized. Whether married or single, working or staying at home, women all across the country have realized how much more effective they could be if they somehow could get organized.

That word *organized* means many things to many people, however. For some it might be putting papers in colored file folders; for others it means putting all their seasonings in alphabetical order. For some it means a clean house, and for others, being able to retrieve papers that have been stored away.

Even after writing 26 books with a combined total of more than 6,000 pages dealing with this topic, I'm not sure I have covered all bases for all women. I have found, though, the following basic steps to be extremely helpful when a person wants to become organized.

- ❧ Start with you. What is it about you that causes you to be disorganized? I find that organized people have a calmness and serenity about them that disorganized people don't have. Search your own self to see what is causing all that confusion. Get rid of that clutter first before you move on.

- ❧ Keep it simple. There are many programs available, but choose one that's simple. You don't want to spend all your time keeping up charts and graphs.

- ❧ Make sure everything has a designated place. One of my sayings is "Don't put it down, put it away." Another, "Don't pile it, file it."

If there is no place for stuff to go, it's going to get piled. And that's one thing you want to prevent—piles.

❧ Store like items together. My husband, Bob, has his gardening supplies and tools together. I have my laundry items in one place, my bill-paying tools in one area, my cups/saucers, my drinking glasses, and my dinnerware all in their general area. Don't spend time going from here to there getting ready for your tasks. Put like items in one place.

❧ Even though you are neat, you may not be organized. I tell women to use notebook organizers and that there are two things to remember. One, write it down; and two, read it. It doesn't do you much good to write down that birthday date or crucial appointment on your calendar and forget both because you didn't read your calendar. Remember to write and read.

❧ Get rid of all items you don't use. They only add to the clutter.

❧ Invest in the proper tools. In order to be organized you need proper tools: bins, hooks, racks, containers, lazy Susans, etc.

❧ Involve the whole family. Learn to delegate jobs and responsibilities to other members of the family. My Bob takes care of all the repairs. When something is broken, he is Mr. Fix-It. Tailor chores to fit the ages of your children. Also, change off frequently so no one gets bored. Most importantly, don't do something yourself that another member of the family can do.

❧ Keep master lists. I've learned to use a three-ring binder, 3" x 5" file cards, and journals to keep track of all our stuff. You may think you'll never forget you loaned that CD to Brad or that video to Christine, but you will. Write it down and keep the list in a place where you cannot overlook it.

❧ Use a lot of labels and signs. If containers, bins, drawers, and shelves aren't labeled, the family won't be able to spot where things go. I have also used color coding to help identify items belonging to various members of the family: blue for Bevan, red for Chad, and purple for Christine. I use a permanent fine-point paint pen very effectively to label clothes, glass and plastic jars, and wooden items.

❧ Continually reevaluate your system. Nothing is written in concrete. It can be changed. See how other people do things, read a book to gather ideas, evaluate your own system. Change when it's not working.

Where to start? Start with these suggestions. Once you have them under control, you're ready for more specific areas. And the first specific area we're going to start with is you.

Emilie

Simply Organized...
For You

How to Feel Personally Organized

Do you ever look around your home, room, or office and just want to throw up your hands in disgust and say, "It's no use. I'll never get organized!" You need not feel that way anymore. With a few simple tools you can feel personally organized.

The old saying, "Everything has a place and everything is in its place," is very helpful to keep in mind. To help you accomplish this you need four tools:

- A "To Do" list
- A calendar
- A telephone/address source list
- A simple filing system

These four tools can drastically change your life from feeling confused to feeling organized.

A "To Do" List

Have the first three of these tools be the same size (8-1/2" x 11" or 8-1/2" x 5-1/2"; etc.). This way you won't have to fight with different sizes of paper. After arriving at your size of paper, write with a regular ink pen the words "To Do" at the top of the page, and begin writing down all the things that are in your head you need to do. As you accomplish each item, you will get so much pleasure in crossing off what's been done. At the end of each day, review your list and update any new things you need to add to your list. At the end of the week consolidate your pages for the week and start again on Monday with a fresh page. As you get more experienced with this list, you will want to rank items by importance. This added technique will help you maximize your time.

A Calendar

I recommend three types of calendars, the first being a two-page month-at-a-glance calendar. At one glance you get a good overview of the month. Details aren't written here, but you do jot down broad descriptions of engagements with times—for example, meetings, lunches, dinners, parties, dentist appointments, etc. The second type of calendar shows an entire week on a two-page format. It should include a small calendar for the month and room for notes on each week's section. The third type of calendar has a page for each day. On this day-at-a-glance calendar you get more detailed and specific and jot down what you will be doing for each hour or half hour.

A Telephone/Address Source List

This listing becomes your personal telephone and address book. (Many daily planners have a place for a list like this.) In this book you design your own directory of information that you will use for home, work, or play. You might want to list certain numbers by broad headings such as: schools, attorneys, dentists, doctors, plumbers, carpenters, restaurants, etc. Broad headings help in looking up the specifics when you can't remember the person's last name.

A Simple Filing System

Adopt this motto: "Don't pile it, file it." This principle will really tidy your area up. Go to your local stationery store and purchase about four dozen 8-1/2" x 14" colored or manila file folders. I recommend colored file folders because they are brighter and add a little cheer to your day. I find that the legal size (8-1/2" x 14") folders are more functional—they can accommodate the longer-sized papers.

On these folders, use simple headings for each: Sales Tax, Auto, Insurance, School Papers, Maps, Warranties, Taxes, Checks, etc. Then take all those loose papers you find around your home and put them in their proper place. Remember: "Don't pile it, file it." If you have a metal file drawer to house these folders, that's great. If not, just pick up a cardboard storage box (the "Perfect Box" with a lid, see page 19) to get started. Later you can move up to a better file cabinet.

Don't you already feel some relief by just reading about these four aids? I hope you do!

A Purse That Works

Pete has just returned with the babysitter, and you're running late for that long-anticipated class reunion. But you want everything to be perfect.

Julie has spilled the cat's milk dish and you're sticking to the kitchen floor, trying to clean up the mess. The phone rings and the rollers are falling out of your hair. "Time—I need more time!" you yell. Pete takes over the cleanup. Your sitter holds baby Jason, and you put Julie in her rocker with a book.

Now it's time for you. Grabbing the cute clutch that matches your outfit, you begin to change purses. As you try to decide what to take out of your everyday bag you begin to wade through the papers, gum wrappers, pacifiers, etc., that have collected in the bottom of your bag. This only gets you upset and frustrated. Dumping the whole contents of the purse on the bed, you say, "Forget it!" Because you're running late, you end up taking your crummy tote bag—which doesn't match your lovely outfit in the least.

End your purse frustrations once and for all. Using these few simple steps, you will be able to change bags and do it quickly. You will never need to hassle with purse-changing again!

Getting Started

What you'll need is a nice-sized purse for everyday use. Then you'll need three to seven little bags. They can be made of quilted fabric (with zipper or Velcro fasteners) or of denim or corduroy prints. Make each little bag different in color and size to identify it more easily. (These little bags can also be purchased.) Your everyday handbag should be pretty good-sized, since it's the one you'll be dragging around with you (and your kids) all over the place. It should be able to hold everything that you'll need.

The Wallet

Find a wallet that's functional for you, because a wallet is very, very important. You want a wallet that has a section where you can keep a few bills and a zipper compartment for change. Keep your most frequently used credit cards, your checkbook, your driver's license, and all those other little important things in your wallet. (You should also keep a pen with your wallet.) Now when you run to the cleaner or the pharmacy to pick something up, rather than taking your big purse with everything in it, all you have to do is pull your wallet out of your purse, run in, and make your little exchange.

The Little Bags

In the little bags you'll keep all sorts of things. One bag holds my sunglasses. In my makeup bags I keep such things as a mirror, lipstick, a small comb, blush, nail clippers, nail file, etc. I also keep some change for an emergency phone call.

In addition to my wallet, sunglasses bag, and makeup bag, I have a bag for reading glasses and two more small bags for various items.

Everything Organized

Suppose your good friend Sue calls you and asks you to lunch. If you decide to go, you can just grab your clutch purse and put a few of the little bags in it. For example, you'll want to take your wallet and credit cards plus your makeup bags. How long will this take you? Not even a minute. You just stick your purse under your arm, and you're off. When you come home again, just take out the little bags and put them back into your everyday purse.

Items for Your Purse

A. Wallet:
   pen, checkbook
   change compartment
   money, credit cards
   driver's license
   calendar (current)
   pictures (most used)

B. Makeup Bag 1:
   lipstick, blush
   comb, small brush
   mirror
   telephone change

C. Makeup Bag 2:
   breath mints, gum, cough drops
   small perfume
   hand cream
   nail clippers
   scissors (small)
   Kleenex
   nail file
   matches

D. Eyeglass case for sunglasses

E. Eyeglass case for reading, spare glasses

F. Small Bag 1:
   business cards (yours and
   your husband's) for:
   - hairdresser
   - doctor (health plan)
   - insurance person
   - auto club
   - seldom-used credit cards
   - tea bag, Sweet 'n' Low, aspirin
   - library card
   - small calculator

G. Small Bag 2:
   small Bible, paperback book
   needle, thread, pins, thimble
   Band-Aid
   collapsible cup
   tape measure
   toothbrush
   toothpicks
   spot remover
   feminine protection

Wardrobe Wonders

Now let's get into our closet and get organized. Let's weed out some of those things we don't need and get our closets in order.

Getting Started

First, we need to get our equipment together. You'll need three trash bags (I suggest using black trash bags so you or your family cannot see what's inside them) and six to twelve boxes which are approximately 16" deep x 12" wide x 10" high with

Equipment You'll Need

❧ 3 trash bags

❧ 6 to 12 Perfect Boxes

❧ 3" x 5" colored index cards

lids. I call these "Perfect Boxes." You'll also need a 3" x 5" card file box with tabbed dividers and 3" x 5" colored index cards.

Now we're ready to get going! Label the trash bags "Put Away," "Give Away," and "Throw Away." Walk into the closet and take everything out.

As you pull items out of your closet, keep in mind that if you haven't worn it for the past year it goes in one of those three bags. Either you're going to put it away somewhere else, or you're going to give it away to somebody else, or you're going to throw it away. If you haven't worn it for two or three years, you'll definitely have to give it away or throw it away.

Taking Inventory

Now let's start taking inventory. (You can use the Wardrobe Inventory sheet printed below.) As you begin to take your inventory, you'll quickly begin to see what you have and need. For example, you may have way too many pairs of navy-blue pants. You only need one pair of good navy-blue pants and maybe a couple pairs of nice jeans. You can begin to see where you've made your mistakes as you take your wardrobe inventory, and you'll be able to start correcting those mistakes.

Wardrobe Inventory

Blouses	Pants	Skirts
Jackets	Sweaters	Dresses
Gowns	Lingerie	Shoes
Jewelry		

Things I Need

Everything in Its Place

Hang your things up as you put them back into your closet. Each thing should have a definite place. For example, all the extra hangers can go at the left end of your closet. Then arrange all your blouses according to color, then your pants, then your skirts, etc. If you have a jacket that matches your pants, separate them. (Hang the jacket with the jackets and the pants with the pants.) This way you can mix or match your things and not always wear the same jacket and pants together.

Suggested order for your clothes:

1) Extra hangers
2) Blouses
3) Pants
4) Skirts
5) Blazers and jackets
6) Sweaters (these can also be folded and put on a shelf or in a drawer)
7) Dresses

Your shoes can go on shoe racks. Some neat different kinds of shoe racks are now available, or you can cover shoeboxes with wallpaper or Christmas paper. (Your children can help you do this.)

Your smaller handbags can go in clear plastic boxes. The larger ones can go up on the shelf above your wardrobe. A hanging plastic shoe bag is great because you can also put your purses and scarves in it. Belts and ties should go on hooks. Or you can just hammer a big nail into the wall. You'd be surprised at how many belts you can get on a nail!

Storage—Put Away Boxes

Get your Perfect Boxes with lids and number each box. Assign each box a 3" x 5" card with a corresponding number. For example:

Box 1—Jenny's summer shorts, T-shirts, skirts, sandals

Box 2—Costume clothing: 1950s outfit, black-and-white saddle shoes, purple angora sweater with holes, high school cheerleader's outfit

Box 3—Ski clothes, socks, long underwear, sweaters, pants

Box 4—Scarves, belts, jewelry, honeymoon peignoir, etc.

File your 3" x 5" cards in their file box behind a tabbed divider marked "Storage." Now, when you want to find your stored ski clothes, you look through your card file and see that they're located in Box 3. What could be easier?

Give Away

Be sure you give away things you're not using. Many people today have limited finances and can't afford some things. If you have clothes that you aren't wearing, give them to someone who will be able to use them. They'll be grateful to you, and you'll feel good about your giving.

Throw Away

Put these items in a trash bag with a twistie on it and set out for the trash.

Now that you've got a good start on feeling personally organized, let's move on to your home. Keep your momentum going and forge ahead.

Simply Organized... At Home

PROPERTY OF
BROADWAY CHRISTIAN CHURCH LIBRARY

Total Mess to Total Rest

Suppose I were to say to you, "Today, I'm going to come home with you. I want you to take me into your house, and I want to go through your closets, to look under your bed, to open your drawers, to look in your pantry, and to go anyplace in your house. I just want to check out your house really well."

Some of you would reply, "Well, that's okay. I've got my house in order, and things are really good there, so you can come over." Others of you would say, "Okay, but don't go into the third bedroom. I've been shoving things in that back bedroom for a long time." Still others of you might say, "There is no way anybody is going to come into my house, because the whole place is a total mess."

Equipment You'll Need

- 3 trash bags
- 6 to 12 Perfect Boxes
- 3" x 5" card file box with tabbed dividers
- 3" x 5" colored index cards—10 cards in 7 different colors
- a filing cabinet (or desk drawer or a Perfect Box) and 10 colored file folders

Controlling Your Home

I am going to show you how to take that mess, no matter what size it is, and turn it into a home that you'll be able to maintain

25

and rest in. You will control your home instead of your home controlling you. We're going to use the same principles we used on your closet, so you've already had some practice.

You'll want to commit yourself to five weeks to unclutter your clutter. I don't want you to become overwhelmed thinking about it, because you're going to take a small portion at a time—only one room a week for the next five weeks. You'll do it nice and slow, so that you'll gradually get your home organized.

It can all be done in 15-minute time slots. On Monday, go into Room 1 and clean like mad for 15 minutes, then forget it until Tuesday and do the same as you did Monday, spending 15 minutes cleaning and organizing. Continue this process throughout the week. Presto! By the end of the week you will have spent one hour and 30 minutes in Room 1. You'll still have Sunday off and a nice, clean, well-organized room. Continue this process until every room in the house is complete.

So start with three large trash bags and label them "Put Away," "Throw Away," and "Give Away." Now visualize yourself standing at the front door with these three big trash bags. Ring the doorbell, then walk through the front door. The first room you come to will be the first room you're going to clean, with the exception of the kitchen. (If that's the room you walk into first, move on. Save the kitchen, because you'll need all the experience you can get before tackling it.) To make it easy, let's say we step into the living room, and on our right is the hall closet.

So we open up the hall closet. We're now going to take everything out of that hall closet. We have to decide to get vicious in making choices about what to do with all the stuff we've taken out of the hall closet. I recommend that you call a friend who would like to help you with your house (and you help with her house). It's great to have a friend because she'll help you make decisions that you haven't been able to make for 15 years.

The Hall Closet

Let's put into the hall closet all those things that actually belong in a hall closet. These include sweaters, coats, umbrella, books, football blanket, binoculars, tennis rackets, etc.

But now we have all these other things that don't belong in there, such as old magazines we've collected for six or seven years. (We were going to look through them some rainy day and cut out the pictures and recipes, but we never did.) So we have to get rid of these things. We've also got papers and receipts and all sorts of other things in that hall closet, so we'll put these either in the Put Away bag, the Throw Away bag, or the Give Away bag.

As we go through our home every week for the next five weeks, we begin to fill up these bags. At the end of the fifth week we may have three, ten, or fifteen bags full of various things. Then we put twisties on the trash bags marked Throw Away and set them out for the trashman. Now they're gone! You've got all those things out of the way.

Now you have two types of bags left: the Give Away bags and the Put Away bags. The Give Away bags will hold things that you may want to hand down to some other family member or to relatives, or clothing that you want to give to a thrift shop, sell at a garage or rummage sale, or donate to your church. And what do you do with the contents of the Put Away bags? Either put the items in their place in the house, or place them in one of your Perfect Boxes. Be sure to note box number and contents on your index file card.

Keeping It Organized

We have our house totally clean. How are we going to maintain it that way? We certainly never want to go through this clutter again! You'll be glad to know we won't have to do it again.

Take your 3" x 5" cards and tabbed dividers. Label the dividers with the following (you already have the "Storage" divider if you went through your wardrobe in the last chapter):

—Daily   —Biannually

—Weekly   —Annually

—Monthly   —Storage

—Quarterly

Assign a color of index cards to each section. On the first set of cards, list those jobs you do daily, such as washing the dishes, making the bed, and picking up around the house. On the next set of cards, list your weekly chores; on the next set, your monthly chores, and so on. Below I've made suggestions for dividing the household tasks.

Daily Chores

Wash dishes   Pick up rooms

Make beds   Pick up kitchen

Check bathrooms

Weekly Chores

Monday—wash, menu plan

Tuesday—iron, water plants

Wednesday—mop floors

Thursday—vacuum, grocery shop

Friday—change bed linens, dust

Saturday—yard work

Sunday—free (except plan for next week!)

Monthly Chores

Week 1—clean refrigerator

Week 2—clean oven

Week 3—wax furniture

Week 4—clean and dust baseboards

Quarterly Chores

Straighten drawers	Dust and straighten china cabinets
Clean windows	Clean cupboards
Clean closets	Move furniture and vacuum
Clean mini-blinds	

Biannual Chores

Clean screens	Rearrange furniture

Annual Chores

Wash curtains	Clean drapes
Clean carpets	Clean out garage/basement/attic
Prune trees	

Now let's say Thursday comes along and your good friend Sue calls and says, "Let's go to lunch, then do some shopping. The department store has a big sale today." So you check your cards and say, "I've done all my daily things, but it's Thursday, so I have to vacuum and go to the market. I can do my marketing this afternoon when we get back, but I don't know about the vacuuming."

You move the vacuuming to Friday, but there's already a list of things to do. So you move those chores to Saturday, but you promised the kids you'd take them to the park. But moving the chores to Sunday isn't going to work either, because you have company coming over after church! By Monday morning you have a million things to do, and the house is already starting to look messy again.

So, you're not going to move the vacuuming to Friday. Instead, you're going to move it to the back of the weekly section. That's right—you're not going to vacuum again until next Thursday, when the vacuuming card comes up again in the file. Rotate the cards daily, whether you do the allotted jobs or not.

By following this system, you avoid cramming a week's worth of housekeeping chores into one day, and you develop a routine that helps keep your priorities in order. When Sue calls next Thursday and invites you to lunch and shopping, you take a look at your unvacuumed floor and say, "How about I meet you at the mall after lunch? I've got a couple of things I need to finish up around here."

Next you have your monthly chores. During Week 1 you clean the refrigerator (you have a whole week to do it, or you can delegate the job to a child). During Week 2 you do the oven, and so forth. This way, every week you're doing a little bit to maintain your home. It's only going to take you a little time, but you're continually maintaining your home so you never have to go through that total mess program again. Next you have your quarterly things to do (straighten drawers, etc.). Then you have your semi-annual tasks (rearrange furniture, wash curtains, etc.). Finally, there are the annual jobs such as cleaning the basement, attic, garage, etc.

Your last tab, at the very back of your file, is your storage tab, which we started when we sorted through the wardrobe. Your 3" x 5" cards are numbered Box 1, Box 2, Box 3, and Perfect Boxes are given a corresponding number. If you want to go a step further, you can make out two cards for each box—one to be pasted on the box and one to go into your card file. Items in your Put Away bags that need to be stored go in these boxes.

Now we take our file box and our colored file folders and look at what's left in our Put Away bags. What do we find? We find old newspaper clippings, warranties, instruction booklets, receipts from car repairs and household repairs, and all kinds of other things. So we put these papers in our colored file folders, label the folders (see the suggested list below), list all those things on 3" x 5" cards, and file the cards away under "Storage" in our file box.

Suggested Labels for Colored File Folders

—Medical

—Warranties

—Insurance papers and booklets

—Car repair receipts

—Appliance instructions

—Special notes, letters, cards

—Decorating ideas

—Receipts from major purchases

What have we done? We've taken a big step toward simply organizing our house—and maintaining that organization. What does that give us? More hours in our day, with no guilt feelings about a cluttered house.

SPEED CLEANING

Here are some helpful tips to make your cleaning go as quickly and smoothly as possible.

1. *Have a good set of cleaning tools on hand.* First-class tools make you feel like you're doing a first-class job. A few items everyone should have:

   - apron
   - feather duster—Invest in an ostrich duster. These are super for moving small amounts of dust from higher levels to lower levels. Use fast but smooth strokes. When finished, shake the duster outside to remove dust from the feathers.
   - pumice stone—Get that ugly ring out of the toilet caused by rust and mineral deposits! It's amazing how fast it will remove the scale. Just rub it on the ring and slosh with water as you rub. Pumice also cleans ovens and removes the carbon build-up on grills and iron cookware.
   - knee pads—Billy's old football knee pads are great protectors for cleaning floors and tubs.
   - toothbrush—to clean the hard corners of areas on floors, showers, and around faucets.
   - whisk broom
   - window/mirror cleaner
   - cloth baby diaper—for cleaning windows.
   - all-purpose cleaner
   - dish cloth—for wet cleaning. Use 100 percent cotton cloths.
   - ammonia—excellent cleaner (not the sudsy type) for floors.
   - oven cleaner
   - rubber gloves

2. *Always start at the top of the room, work down and around.* Mop or vacuum last.

3. *Go in one direction.* Work around your room from top to bottom and from right to left (or left to right). Always start at one end of your home and work toward the other end. Don't get sidetracked with this mess and that mess.

4. *Put on some music with a very fast beat.* This will help your cleaning go faster plus take your mind off the drudgery.

5. *Work in 15-minute increments.* Set your kitchen timer for 15 minutes and work like crazy until it goes off. You'll be surprised at how much you can accomplish!

6. *Try to avoid interruptions.* Let the answering machine take phone messages and call back when it's convenient.

7. *Use these speed-cleaning tips.*

   - Before cleaning window panes, wipe or vacuum sills and wood cross frames. With your window cleaner and baby diaper, use a horizontal stroke on the outside and a vertical stroke on the inside. If you miss a spot, you'll be able to tell which side of the window it's on.

   - Use your feather duster to dust silk flowers, soft fabric items, plants, picture frames, lampshades, windowsills, bookshelves, and door frames. (Since you're working top to bottom, you'll be vacuuming up this dust soon.)

   - After wiping your wastebaskets clean, give the inside bottom a quick coat of floor wax. This will prevent trash from sticking to the bottom of the wastebasket in the future.

   - Change your air conditioner and heater filters every six months, and wipe off the blades of your window and/or room fans quarterly. This will keep the dust and dirt from circulating through your rooms.

8. *Make big tasks into smaller tasks.* If cleaning the refrigerator seems overwhelming, clean the bottom shelf on Monday, the middle shelf on Tuesday, the fruit and vegetable drawers on Wednesday, and the outside on Thursday. Big projects become more manageable when broken into smaller parts.

9. *Don't forget to treat yourself for a job well done.* After you finish a task, enjoy a cup of coffee or tea, or put on a face masque and take a hot bath—whatever you find rewarding for your labors!

Getting Your Kitchen Under Control

Do you realize that one of the reasons you're desperate for kitchen organization is because you spend an average of 1,092 hours a year in the kitchen? That's a lot of hours in an area that definitely needs to be organized.

Getting Started

First you'll need some jars. Tupperware is a wonderful thing to have as well. Those lazy Susan turntables are also super. Also get Contact paper, newspapers, or anything that you can cover some boxes with. You'll also need trash bags, plus a felt-tip marker pen and some labels.

Scheduling Time

The next crucial thing is to schedule a time. Here's what I recommend: Set the timer on your stove for 15 minutes, then work like mad until the timer goes off. Then do whatever else you have to. If you're working toward a deadline, you have a tendency to move a little faster. So schedule yourself a time in the day when you're going to organize your kitchen.

Equipment You'll Need

- jars
- Tupperware
- lazy Susans
- Perfect Boxes labeled "Kitchen Overflow"
- Contact paper to match the colors of your kitchen
- trash bags marked "Throw Away" and "Give Away"
- felt-tip pen
- labels

First Stop: the Cupboards

First, let's open all cupboard doors. Starting with the cupboards closest to the sink (because these are the ones we get in and out of the most and that are probably in the biggest mess), pull everything out. Wipe out the shelves and repaper with Contact paper if needed.

Now for the things you're not using, such as broken dishes, mugs, vases, plus cleansers and other things that are partially used but you'll never use again. Put these in either your Throw Away bag, your Give Away bag, or a Perfect Box marked "Kitchen Overflow." These seldom-used boxes can be stored on the garage shelves or where you have extra room.

The things you don't use very often should go back in the cupboards, but on the highest shelves. This might include such things as big platters for your Thanksgiving turkey. (You might use this only once or twice a year.)

Items that you use daily go back into the cupboards in easily accessible places. Such things as spices, dishes, pots and pans, etc., should be put back neatly. I use lazy Susan turntables for my spices, or you can use a spice rack. (A spice rack or a lazy Susan also comes in handy for vitamin bottles.)

Get your broken appliances repaired. They're sitting around waiting for somebody to pay attention to them. Those that would

> *Helpful Hint:*
>
> Glue a 12-inch square of cork to the inside of the cabinet door over your kitchen work area. On the cork tack the recipe card you are using and newspaper clippings of recipes you plan to try within a few days. It keeps them at eye level, and they stay splatter-free.

cost more than half the cost of a new appliance to repair should be thrown out.

For those of you who have high school students going to college, put your extra appliances in a box and store them away. When our children went off to college and started getting their own apartments, they wanted such things as the extra iron, toaster, etc. So label them and number them. Then put this information in your card files.

> *Helpful Hint:*
> Mark your storage bowls and their covers with the same number, using a marking pen. Then you won't always be looking for the bowl when you're putting away leftovers. All you have to do is match the numbers.

Kitchen Overflow

Now for your overflow. At one time Bob and I and the children lived in a condominium. We had moved from a big two-story house to a small three-bedroom condominium. I found that when I was organizing the kitchen I didn't have a place for everything. That's when I discovered what I call the kitchen overflow. If you're lucky enough to have a shelf or cabinets in the garage, that's a good place to put the overflow. If not, get some boxes with lids and put the overflow in them. The overflow might include such things as a waffle iron, an extra set of dishes, or even extra canned goods.

What can you do with gadgets and utensils if you're short on space? Put them in a crock and tie a little bow around it. The crock looks cute on the counter, and all your whips and wooden spoons and spatulas can probably fit in it. Set the crock close to the stove or at some other handy spot.

Unavoidable Junk

Then there are the junk drawers. There is no way to eliminate these, so don't feel you have to get rid of those junk drawers. We all have them. The problem is, they are usually very junky. But we can take that junk and pretty well clean it up. My junk drawer has a little silverware sectional container. In it I put the hammer, the screwdriver, and a couple of those small artichoke jars in which I keep some cup hooks, nails, screws, and thumbtacks—all those little things. You may want to get two or three jars to put in your junk drawer so you'll have everything fairly organized when you pull it out.

Pantry Stocking List

Date_____

Qty.	Cost	Starches	Qty.	Cost	Canned & Bottled Goods	Qty.	Cost	
___	___	Flour	___	___	Tuna	___	___	Brown Mustard
___	___	Cornmeal	___	___	Juices	___	___	Yellow Mustard
___	___	Oatmeal	___	___	Peanut Butter	___	___	Oil
___	___	Pasta	___	___	Tomato Sauce	___	___	Tabasco Sauce
___	___	White Rice	___	___	Tomato Paste	___	___	Worcestershire
___	___	Brown Rice	___	___	Dried Fruit	___	___	Sauce
___	___	Potatoes	___	___	Dried Mixes (i.e. Salad Dressing, Taco Mix)			
			___	___	Canned Vegetables			**Perishable Foods**
			___	___	Canned Fruit	___	___	Fresh Garlic
		Sweet-Based Staples	___	___	Pancake Mix	___	___	Ginger
___	___	Brown Sugar	___	___	Jello	___	___	Green Peppers
___	___	White Sugar	___	___	Pudding Mix	___	___	Celery
___	___	Powdered Sugar	___	___	Soup	___	___	Eggs
___	___	Honey				___	___	Nuts
___	___	Maple Syrup				___	___	Green Onions
___	___	Jams/Jellies				___	___	Yellow Onions
___	___					___	___	White Onions
						___	___	Tomatoes
					Condiments	___	___	Carrots
			___	___	Ketchup	___	___	White Cheese
			___	___	Vinegar	___	___	Yellow Cheese
			___	___	Capers	___	___	Lemons

Another handy organizer is an egg carton. This is fabulous to use for those little screws. You can cut apart the cartons so that you have small sections of egg cartons. Then the screws, hooks, etc., can fit in there and go nicely in your junk drawer.

Pantry Space

Even if you don't have a pantry, you may have a cupboard in your kitchen that you're using as a pantry. The pantry can be organized in a really fun and cute way. Organize your staples and canned goods by category. For example, put canned fruit in one row and dry cereal in another. To help keep your food items in the right place, label your pantry shelves accordingly.

Put packaged items, such as dried taco mix, salad dressings, gravies, etc., into a large jar or small shoebox covered with wallpaper or contact paper. You can also purchase plastic or metal sliding shelves.

Put everything you can in jars—rice, Bisquick, popcorn, beans, sugar, flour, graham crackers, cookies, raisins, coffee filters, dog biscuits.

As you plan your weekly menus, check your staple and perishable foods and replenish if necessary.

Work Together, Store Together

Things that work together should be stored together. What does this mean? If you're going to organize baking items—your mixing bowls, your hand mixer, your measuring cups—all those things can be stored in one small area together. I bake homemade bread, so I have on my shelf all those things that I use to bake the bread. I have my pans, the oil, the honey, the flour, the yeast, etc.,

Helpful Hint:

Plan a "cooking marathon" with a friend or your family. Bake or cook a few entries such as breads, cakes, casseroles, and soups. Freeze the items, some in family portions and some in individual servings, and date and label each item. Now, on a day when Mom's sick or there's no time to cook a meal, you can open up your freezer and take your pick!

handy, so that when I'm ready to bake bread I don't have to be running from cupboard to cupboard trying to find things. Coffeepot, filters, coffee, and even mugs could also be stored together.

Put kitchen towels and cloths in a drawer or on a shelf close to the sink. Keep pot holders near point of use.

Pots and Pans

Pots and pans should be kept neatly somewhere near the stove. You can line the shelves for the pots with plain or light-colored paper—maybe brown paper. Determine the best possible position for your pans, because those are things you use often and need to get out quickly. You can draw a circle or square the size of the pan with a black felt pen, then write the pan size inside the circle or square. For example, here is where the nine-inch frying pan goes and that's where the two-quart saucepan goes. If you have people other than yourself doing things in your kitchen, this is a wonderful way for them to know where things are to be stored.

The Refrigerator

What about the refrigerator? Look at that refrigerator as just another closet, because basically that's what it is—a cold-storage closet. Fruits and vegetables should be put in plastic containers with lids, plastic bags, or refrigerator drawers. Cheese and meats go on the coldest shelf. Use all types of see-through containers with tight lids.

Lazy Susans are great space-savers in your refrigerator. I have two of them. One is on the top shelf and stores the milk and the half-and-half. The other one has the sour cream, the cottage cheese, etc.

You can also buy dispensers and bottle racks for your refrigerator. Can dispensers are good if you use a lot of soft drinks. Some dispensers you can set right onto the shelf in your refrigerator, and they dispense from there. There are also special milk dispensers, juice dispensers, and so forth. Your children will absolutely love these.

At least once a year pull the plug on your refrigerator and give it a thorough cleaning with baking soda (one tablespoon baking soda to one quart water). Let it air dry.

The Freezer

Now what about the freezer? All your frozen vegetables should be put in one section and your meats in another section. All your casseroles that you premake can also be put together. When I make a lasagna casserole or spaghetti sauce, I make enough for that night plus one for the freezer. And I always label and date containers so I'll know how long they've been in the freezer. If you are freezing in jars, leave 1/2" at the top to allow for expansion.

I also try to keep emergency meals in the freezer in case company drops in or I've been too busy to prepare anything else. You can buy plastic containers

Helpful Hint:
Do not store cookies, cereal, or other "bait" by the stove. Children can get burned climbing on the stove to reach an item overhead.

especially for making TV dinners. With these, if you have leftovers from the meal, you can put together one TV dinner with foil around the top, then label it and put it into the freezer. When you get four or five of these accumulated, you've got a nice meal for everyone that's just a little different.

Be sure you label dishes that go into the freezer, because otherwise you'll find mystery packages in the freezer as you clean it out. It's amazing how things don't look the same when they're frozen!

Ice cream and frozen desserts should go together in your freezer. Did you know that you can freeze potato chips, corn chips, tortillas, muffins, and bread? If you use wheat flour, be sure to keep that in the freezer so it will keep nice and fresh. Candles should also be kept in the freezer. (If you keep them in the freezer, they won't drip or pop when you light them.)

Meal Planning

For simple and easy to prepare meals, take a look at the recipes and menu suggestions starting on page 95.

Ten Benefits of Meal Planning

1. Saves you time
2. Saves you money
3. Saves you stress
4. Prevents making bad choices
5. Gives you better nutrition
6. Makes happy homes
7. Makes happy meals
8. Makes happy children
9. Makes happy husbands
10. Makes a very happy mom who has a very happy family!

Kitchen Basics

No matter how large or small, any kitchen can be tailored to suit your lifestyle. Here are some basic utensils to have on hand to make your culinary pursuits that much easier.

Pots and Pans
- one 10" skillet with lid
- a set of covered casserole dishes
- a roasting pan with rack
- bread pans
- two cookie sheets
- double boiler
- one muffin pan with 6 to 12 cups
- Dutch oven or similar type of pan

Optional Gadgets
- grater
- colander
- sifter
- vegetable steamer
- food grinder
- eggbeater
- whisk
- egg slicer

Larger Gadgets
- mixer
- blender
- food processor
- toaster oven
- microwave oven
- freezer
- slow cooker

Other Necessities
- a good set of knives
- a steel knife sharpener
- a set of measuring cups
- wooden spoons
- a mallet
- rubber spatula
- shears
- rolling pin
- storage bowls
- cheese slicer
- tongs
- garlic press

Setting Up a Desk and Work Area

As I began to get my home in order and to eliminate all the clutter, I soon realized that I didn't have an area to handle all the mail and paper that came into our home. It wasn't easy to follow our motto, "Don't put it down, put it away." We had piles of paper stacked in no organized fashion.

We soon realized we needed a central desk or work area in order to function properly with maximum effectiveness. Paper handling depends on a good physical setup in a practical location furnished with a comfortable working surface and a good inventory of supplies. Ideally, this office will become a permanent fixture where the business procedures of your home are done. The area should have access to supplies and files and be located where other household operations do not interfere. However, if your desk/work area can't be this ideal, don't let it stop you from getting started.

Since a desk or work area is so basic to a smoothly functioning lifestyle, here are some practical steps for setting up this area in your home.

Choosing the Location

In order to help you choose that ideal setting, you might ask yourself these questions:

- ❦ Do you need to be in a place where it's quiet, or is it better for you to be near people?

❧ Do big windows distract you, or do you like being near windows?

❧ Do you prefer a sunny room or a shaded one?

❧ Do you prefer to work in the morning or in the afternoon?

The answer to these questions helps narrow your alternatives. Walk around your home to see which areas meet the answers to your four questions. After selecting at least two locations, you might ask yourself another set of questions:

❧ Is there enough space for your computer?

❧ Are there enough electrical outlets and telephone jacks?

❧ Is there enough space for a desk?

❧ Is this location out of the way of other household functions? If not, can they be shifted so they won't interfere with your office hours?

Again, add the answers to these questions to your previously selected alternatives and narrow them down to a final selection. Do you feel good about this selection? Live with it a few days before making a final decision.

Selection of Desk, Equipment, and Supplies

After you have selected the location for your office, you need to take a sheet of paper and make a diagram of the floor plan. You will use this information when you want to make or select furniture for your new work area.

The Desk

❧ Writing surface: Your desk should be sturdy and comfortable to use, with a surface that doesn't wobble.

❧ Place for supplies: Have at least one large drawer in which paper and envelopes can be kept in folders. If you find a desk with large drawers on each side, so much the better. There needs to be a shallow drawer with compartments for paper clips, rubber bands, and other supplies. At your local stationery store you can purchase small trays with dividers that can store these small items.

ಈ Files and records: A home office seldom has need for more than one file drawer. If your desk has at least one drawer big enough to contain letter-size folders (legal-size is preferable), all your files will probably be comfortably accommodated.

ಈ Typing/computer platform: If you have a typewriter or a personal computer and plan to use it in your work area, try to get a desk with a built-in platform for these to rest on. If you have enough room in your office, you might want to designate a separate area in your office for typing and computer work.

Other Storage Ideas

ಈ Wall organizers are helpful for pads, pens, calendars, and other supplies.

ಈ Paper, pencils, and supplies can be kept in stackable plastic or vinyl storage cubes under the desk.

ಈ Use an extra bookcase shelf to store a laptop computer, basket of supplies, or some files.

ಈ Use stackable plastic bins that can be added to for your expanded needs. Use the small style for stationery and papers, and a larger size (a vegetable bin) for magazines and newspapers.

Supplies

ಈ Address book or Rolodex—I personally like both. The address book I take with me when traveling or on business, and I keep a Rolodex permanently housed on my desk. The Rolodex also has more room for adding other information you might want to use when addressing that particular person/business.

ಈ Appointment calendar—Ideally the calendar should be small enough to carry around, as well as for use at your desk. If you search around, you can find a combination notebook and calendar that isn't too bulky to carry around in your briefcase or handbag. The date squares should be large enough to list appointments comfortably. See page 12.

❦ Bulletin board—This is a good place to collect notes and reminders to yourself.

❦ Business cards—a must time-saver

❦ Desk lamp

❦ Dictionary

❦ File folders—I use colored "third-cut" folders in which the stick-up tabs are staggered so they don't block each other from view. The colors give a more attractive appearance to your file drawer.

❦ Letter opener

❦ Marking pens—It is useful to have on hand a few marking pens in different colors. I do a lot of color-coding on my calendar. I also use a yellow highlighter pen when I want some information to pop out at me for rereading.

❦ Paper clips—small and large

❦ Postcards—save money on your mailing

❦ Pencil sharpener

❦ Pencils and pens

❦ Postage scale—a small, inexpensive type

❦ Rubber bands—mixed sizes

❦ Rubber stamp and ink pad—There are all kinds of rubber stamps you can use in your office. These are much cheaper than printed stationery or labels. If you use a certain one over and over, you might consider having a self-inking stamp made for you—it's a great time-saver.

❦ Ruler

❦ Scissors

- ❧ Scratch paper—Use lined pads for this. "Post-It Notes" are also great.

- ❧ Scotch tape and dispenser

- ❧ Stamps—In addition to regular stamps, keep appropriate postage on hand for additional weight and special handling if you do these types of mailings regularly.

- ❧ Stapler, staples, staple remover

- ❧ Stationery and envelopes—Usually the 8-1/2" x 11" plain white paper with matching business-size envelopes is all you will need. I find 9" x 6" and 9" x 12" manila envelopes are good for mailing bulk documents, books, or magazines. Sometimes a #6 Jiffy padded envelope is useful to ship items that need some protection from rough handling in transit.

- ❧ Telephone—An extension right at your desk is great. I use my cordless telephone for this, and it works just fine.

You now have an office space that can function to meet your maximum needs. This addition to your lifestyle should certainly make you more efficient in other areas of your life. It will give you a feeling of accomplishment.

Helpful Hint:
Decorative objects such as a ceramic mug look attractive holding pencils and pens.

How to Manage Your Mail

Most of us can't wait for the mail to come each day, but often the thought of processing it all is overwhelming. I've discovered three easy steps that have helped me manage my mountains of mail. I hope they work for you, too!

1. *Designate one area where you open and process all your mail.* It could be a desk, a table by a chair, or the kitchen counter. If you use the kitchen counter, however, be careful not to use it as a catchall. Have a recycle bin or trash can nearby.

2. *Don't let it pile up!* Set a time each day (and I stress the "each day") when you process your mail. If you can't get to it when you receive your mail, then plan a time when you can.

3. *Make decisions.* Don't put it down; put it away. And don't be a mail scooter. It's easy to scoot mail from one area to another, one room to the next, or from one pile to another. Sort out your mail into categories:

   ❦ *Throwaway mail*—junk mail, advertisements, etc. Junk mail is a time waster, so toss it! Don't let yourself say, "I'll probably use this someday," because you very likely will *not*.

   ❦ *Mail you need to read,* but don't have time for now. I slip mail such as newsletters and magazines into a file folder and take the file folder along with me in the car. When I have to wait, in the doctor's office, for children, or even in a long line, I use that time to catch up on my mail reading.

   ❦ *Mail you need to file away,* such as bills, insurance papers, and receipts.

- ❦ *Mail you need to ask someone about*—husband, children, etc. Make notes or question marks so both of you can discuss it.

- ❦ *Mail that needs action.* Sometimes you have a question or need a clearer explanation than the letter gave, or you receive an address change that needs to be noted. Sort such mail together and plan a time to work through it.

- ❦ *Mail to be answered*—personal letters, forms to be filled out and returned, RSVPs for invitations. As a common courtesy to your host, an RSVP should be answered as soon as you know your plans. Mark dates on your calendar when the invitations arrive.

Helpful Hint:

Personal mail goes to the person. When the children were home, all personal mail went into the folder of each individual member of the Barnes family and went directly to the person's work station. This might be a desk, a kitchen table, or his or her bed. This way we could all find our daily mail.

All these categories can be labeled on file folders and put into a file box or metal file cabinet. As soon as the mail comes in, simply slip it into its proper place.

Your mail *can* be managed! This is one of the easiest (and most rewarding) steps to a simply organized life.

Don't Be a Paperwork Slave

Every day we make decisions about paper—from personal mail to children's schoolwork, newspapers to magazines, receipts to warranties. If you find yourself buried in years of collected, often-forgotten papers, there's hope! I have six simple steps to free you from the slavery of paperwork.

1. Schedule set times for sorting through papers. Doing a little each day will help to ward off paper chaos.

2. Collect materials you will need to help you get organized.

   - metal file cabinet or file boxes
   - plastic trash bags
   - file folders
   - black felt marking pen

3. Start with whatever room annoys you the most. Work your way through every pile of paper. Go through closets and drawers. When you finish a room, move on to the next.

4. Throw away.

   - Be determined. Make decisions. Throw away the clutter.
   - Perhaps you have lots of articles, recipes, or children's school papers and artwork which you have been saving for that special "someday."
   - Keep the saving of papers to a minimum. Put the throwaway papers into bags and carry them out to the trash. Don't wait. It's a good feeling!

53

❧ Don't get bogged down rereading old letters, recipes, articles, etc. It's easy to spend too much time reminiscing and get sidetracked from your purpose of streamlining your paper-filing system.

❧ Keep legal papers a minimum of seven years.

❧ If you have trouble determining what to throw away, ask a friend to help you make some of those decisions. Friends tend to be more objective, and you can return the favor when they decide to clean up their clutter.

5. File.

❧ Categorize the papers you want to save (for example, magazine articles, family information, IRS papers, bank statements/canceled checks, charge accounts, utilities, taxes, house, and investment).

❧ Within each category, mark a folder or envelope for each separate account. In the utilities, for example, you would have water, gas, electric, and the telephone. In the insurance folder it is helpful to designate separate envelopes for life, health, car, and house insurance.

❧ Label a folder for each member of the family. These can be used for keeping health records, report cards, notes, drawings, awards, and other special remembrances.

❧ Other suggestions for categories: vacation possibilities, Christmas card lists, home improvement ideas, warranties, instruction booklets, photos/negatives, and car/home repair receipts.

❧ File papers at the time they are received.

❧ Place files in cabinet or boxes.

6. Store.

    ❦ Store files in a closet, garage, attic, or some other area that is out of sight yet easily accessible.

    ❦ Be sure to label the file boxes. If you have set up the storage system I talked about in earlier chapters, you can note on your 3" x 5" cards the contents of each box. Make a note of where that box is stored.

> *Helpful Hint:*
> *One of the stresses of paper is that we put it down and end up with piles all over the house. Make a designated area for all papers and use it.*

You can be free from the piles of paperwork cluttering your house! Take these simple steps and start today.

Remember: Don't pile it—file it.

Shortcuts to Sanity

Through the years I've collected hundreds of helpful hints to make your home more organized and your life a little easier. On the following pages you'll find some of my favorite ideas and charts to ease you through every busy day.

Group Your Shopping Trips Together

In your daily planner keep a list of items you need to buy: books, videos, Christmas gifts, clothes, cosmetics, housewares, birthday, and anniversary gifts. When you see a sale or go to an outlet store, you can acquire what's on your list. This will save time and a lot of money later.

Purchase More Than One Like Item

If you have frequent demands for items like toiletries, pens, rulers, tape, and scissors, store several of each in strategic spots around the house. Don't waste time running all over the house to obtain a basic item.

Plan on Doing More Than One Thing at a Time

Most women can do more than one thing at a time very easily with a little training. Using a cordless phone, I can do any number of things while talking to a friend or relative. I often carry along a few notecards while I'm running errands so I can write a friend if I find myself waiting for something. If you're into exercise and you have an indoor exercise machine, this is a great time to read your favorite book as you work out on your treadmill.

Use Your Body Clock

Each of us operates most efficiently at a certain time of day. Schedule taxing chores for the hours when your mind is sharpest. Do these chores when you have the most energy.

Store Your Keys and Glasses in One Area

My Bob used to always waste time looking for the car keys and his glasses. One day I put up a decorative key hook by the phone in the kitchen and told him to put his car keys on the hook and to place his glasses on the counter underneath the keys. Done deal—no more problem.

Have It Picked Up and Delivered

We're returning to the good old days. More and more companies are offering these services. They are a valuable time-saver, and in many situations they are cost-efficient.

Become a List Maker

In my daily planner I have a list for almost everything I do— from planning a tea for a group of friends to planning a Christmas party for 75 people. I save these notes so next time I can go back and review my comments. It's a great way to start planning since you already have a good beginning.

Plan Your Errands

Do the whole group at one time. My Bob is the greatest at this. I'm continually amazed at how much he gets accomplished when he leaves to run errands. He has his list in hand, with the order of his stops. Within a short time he's back and I'm throughly impressed.

Stop Procrastinating

Start the engine and get in motion. Even if all your ducks aren't lined up, get moving. A car has to be moving in order for it to go somewhere. Start now!

It Doesn't Have to Be Perfect

This goes hand in hand with procrastination—not wanting to do something if it's not perfect. It's nice to want things done right, but not if you are crippled into inactivity. You may know the difference, but your friends and guests won't know it's not perfect. Some jobs don't need perfection. Just do it.

Shop Once for Greeting Cards

Rather than going out 15 or 20 times during the year, I spend 30 minutes to an hour once or twice a year at a card shop. I take the sheet labeled "Dates and Occasions" to help me pick out the cards for everyone that I'm going to need to send a card to throughout the year. (See p. 65.) Along with that I'll add some anniversary cards, get-well cards, and sympathy cards. Then I file all the cards in file folders marked "Greeting Cards."

The Gift Shelf

Somewhere in your home it's nice to have a gift shelf. At any of the department store sales, pick up a few nice items—a box of stationery, little teddy bears, or whatever is useful. I've always had a gift shelf in my home. When the children had a birthday party to go to, I would let them go pick out what they wanted from the shelf to give to Bradley Joe or Weston or whomever. This way you've got something right there, and you don't have to run out to a department store, spending a lot of time and money.

The Gift Wrap Shelf

It saves time and money to have a gift wrap shelf (or box or drawer). Once a year I'll go to where they have gift wrap on sale.

On your gift wrap shelf you should have some colored ribbon, Scotch tape, scissors, and a few dried or silk flowers to put on a package. You should also have some mailing labels and strapping tape.

The Family History Chart

Here you can list your children's names, their birth dates, their blood types, dates of their yearly physical, their dental exams, their eye exams, when they had their inoculations, etc. Everything is nicely listed here so you can refer back to it.

Family History

Family Member Name	Birth Date	Blood Type	Date of Last:			Inoculation Date	Other
			Yearly Physical	Dental Exam	Eye Exam		

Shopping Guide Chart

The family Shopping Guide Chart is a practical way of knowing how your family grows. This will enable you to quickly give grandparents and family members children's clothing sizes.

Shopping Guide

Family Member Name	Sizes					Favorite Activities	Other Clubs Interests, Etc.
	Dress/Suit	Shoes	Pants	Socks	Underwear		

The Credit Cards Sheet

List the name of the company, the account number, the address, the telephone number, and when the card expires. Then, if it's lost or stolen, you can quickly go to your notebook and report it immediately. If you do some purchasing over the telephone or on the Internet, you have the number handy, and you won't have to fumble through your purse trying to find your credit card.

Credit Cards

Company	Card Number	Company Address	Company Phone Number	Card Expires (Date)

The Important Numbers Sheet

List phone numbers for the police, the fire department, the ambulance service, the poison control service, the neighbors, etc.

Important Numbers

Service Person	Phone Number	Service Person	Phone Number
Ambulance		Neighbor	
Appliance Repair		Newspaper	
Dentist		Orthodontist	
Doctor		Pastor	
Electrician		Poison Control	
Fire		Police	
Gardener		Pool Service	
Gas Co. Emergency		Plumber	
Glass Repair		School(s)	
Heating/Air Conditioning Repair Person		School(s)	
Husband's Work		Veterinarian	
Insurance (Car)		Cat's Name	
Insurance (Home)		Dog's Name	

Dates and Occasions

List everybody's birthday, everybody's anniversary, and all the other important dates for the year. As each month comes up, check to see whose birthday is listed. You can show on the chart if you sent a card or what kind of gift you gave last year.

Dates and Occasions

Month	Date/ Occasion	Name of Person(s)	Gift(s) Given	Month	Date/ Occasion	Name of Person(s)	Gift(s) Given
January				July			
February				August			
March				September			
April				October			
May				November			
June				December			

The Home Instructions Sheet

The next time you have someone housesit or take care of your children while you're away, leave a Home Instructions Sheet. You can note your weekly routine as well as things like trash pick up. Maybe your mother-in-law sees this man walking around in your backyard one day, and she doesn't know who he is. She can check the Home Instructions Sheet and say, "That's the pool man, or that's the gardener, so I'm not going to worry about him."

Home Instructions

	Routine Chores/Errands	Special Appointments
Sunday		
Monday		
Tuesday		
Wednesday		
Thursday		
Friday		
Saturday		

The Item Loaned List

For many years I loaned items to friends, thinking I would surely remember who had my turkey platter, Tupperware bowls, picnic basket, and the children's sleeping bags. You know what? I forgot after a short period of time! This simple form makes it easy to keep track of what you've loaned.

Items Loaned List

Month/Year

Date	Item	Who	Returned

The On Order List

Have you ever forgotten what you've ordered from your favorite catalog? Or which manufacturer's rebate coupons you have sent in? Spend a few minutes recording those "on-order" items that need to be tracked until they have been received.

On Order List

Date Ordered	Item	Company	Date Due	Received

Love Baskets

One of the joys of cleaning up the clutter is having time to do the special things you *want* to do. For me, creating little surprises for the people in my life who I love is something I *now* have time for. One of my favorite treats is what I call "Love Basket." It can be filled with food for dinner at the beach, or it can be taken to a ball game. It can even be taken in your car on a love trip. It may be a surprise lunch or dinner in the backyard, in your bedroom, or under a tree, but be creative and use it to say "I love you."

What You'll Need

Here are the things you'll need in order to make a Love Basket. First of all, you'll need a basket with a handle, preferably a heavy-duty basket something like a picnic basket without a lid. Then you'll need a tablecloth, about 45" square. You'll want to line the inside of your basket with this tablecloth, letting it drape over the sides so it looks real cute. I make these for wedding shower gifts, anniversary gifts, or bridal gifts.

Inside the basket put two fancy glasses with stems. You'll also need four napkins. I like to use one with a small print, or maybe a gingham, to make the basket look fun and different. One napkin will be for the lap and the other will be used as a napkin, but for now fluff up your napkins inside the top of the glasses so they puff up and look like powder puffs inside your glasses.

Next you'll need to add a nice tall candle holder and a candle. I like to use something tall because it shows over the top of the basket. You'll also need a bottle of sparkling apple cider. You'll want a loaf of French bread, plus some pretty fresh flowers to make the basket look fun and inviting. Also, you'll want some cheese, salami, dill pickles, and any other good things that you really like.

I've been making Love Baskets for my husband for more than 48 years. We all sense times when our husband needs a little extra attention. Maybe things have been tough at work, or maybe he's depressed over something, or maybe he just needs to feel that he's needed. These are times when you want to put together a Love Basket.

I can remember saying to a friend or neighbor, "You know, my Bob needs a Love Basket tomorrow night, and I'd like to do it for him. Would you take the kids for a few hours for me? The next time your husband needs a Love Basket, I'll take your kids for you." I tell you, they're happy to do it for you. And I'm happy to do it for anyone.

One Valentine's Day Bob and I weren't going to be able to be together, so I decided I would make a Love Basket for him the night before. That morning I called him at work and said, "Tonight I want to take you out to a special restaurant that you've never been to before that has your very favorite food." He asked, "Well, where is it?" I replied, "I'm not going to tell you. It's just a special place in town that I'm going to take you tonight. Could you be home by six o'clock?" Do you know what? He got home at 5:30!

What he didn't know was that during the morning I had fried his very favorite Southern fried chicken. I had also made potato salad, fruit salad, and some yummy rolls. I had the whole dinner prepared in the morning because I didn't want the house to smell from food and give away the surprise when he walked in the door that night.

Love Baskets add a special touch to any occasion—and they're simple to do.

How to Get More Hours in Your Day

Start Your Day the Night Before

- ❦ Set the breakfast table the night before.
- ❦ Gather laundry and sort it.
- ❦ Set up the coffeepot for morning.
- ❦ Make a list of what must be done the next day.

Get Up Early

- ❦ The last one out of the bed makes the bed!
- ❦ Put in the first load of wash.
- ❦ Shower and dress.

Advance to the Kitchen

- ❦ Rejoice that the table is set and attractive.
- ❦ Prepare breakfast.
- ❦ Call everyone to the table with a "two-minute warning."
- ❦ Have everyone take their dishes to the sink when through.
- ❦ Put all dishes in the sink to soak in hot water.
- ❦ Check your "To Do" list.

Put Your Day in Full Swing

- ❦ Have each child check his or her room.
- ❦ Check the bathroom for clothes and cleanliness.
- ❦ Have your children check for their lunch or money, books, homework, gym clothes, etc.

Get Back to Work or Off to Work

- ❦ Put in a second load of wash.
- ❦ Do the dishes.
- ❦ Do any advance dinner preparation.
- ❦ Clean up the counters.
- ❦ Rejoice that your basic housework is done!
- ❦ Check your "To Do" list.

Prepare Your Home for the Evening

- ❦ Prepare munchies if dinner is a bit late.
- ❦ Start to unwind and think toward a quiet, gentle spirit.
- ❦ Organize the children as best as you possibly can.
- ❦ Do not share the negative part of the day with your family until after dinner.
- ❦ Enjoy your family.

Simply Organized...
Especially for Kids

Children Need to Be Organized, Too

When my children were young, I can honestly say that their ideas and my ideas of organization were completely different—like North Pole and South Pole! There were a few ideas that did work, though, and I'm sure they'll work for you. (I'm also happy to report that both my children, now grown, are more organized than I am in some areas!)

The Children's File Box

When our children were about 12 or 13 years old, I set up a file box for each of them. (I wish I had done it even earlier). I gave them ten file folders, and one day we went through their rooms and organized. They began to file all their report cards, all their special reports, and all their pictures and letters. Jenny was lucky enough to get some love letters, so she filed those in her file box. She also pressed and filed the flowers from her special dates and proms. When she got her first car, the insurance papers all went into the file box.

When the children went away to college, the first thing they took with them was their file box. It had all their important papers. When they came home for the summer, home came the file box. When Jenny was married, she took her file box with her. All her little treasures were in that box. Then she got another box and ten more file folders, and she set up a household file box. So now she has all those warranties, instruction booklets, and insurance papers in her household file.

Other Great Ideas for Organizing the Kids

- ❧ Keep those socks sorted by pinning them together with a safety pin or clipping them together with clothespins. Put the child's initials on the socks with a black paint pen.

- ❧ Review the family calendar together. On Sunday evening we would go over our large desktop calendar to see where we were all going to be during the coming week. Were there any transportation or babysitting needs—any church activities, birthday parties, holidays, etc.? Is all homework ready for Monday at school? Any gifts needed for the week? This lets us touch bases and make sure we were all on the same schedule.

- ❧ Have one area where the children place all their school items. I used colored bins by the front door where each child would put his/her gym clothes, homework, schoolbooks. This saved a lot of last-minute hunting for items before running off to school.

- ❧ Have a dress-up box available for those spontaneous plays that your children perform on days they play inside because of weather. Today I use these old clothes for the grandchildren when they come over to play.

- ❧ Have a box of games, toys, and coloring books to take with you on long trips. Also bring along an old sheet and spread it on the back seat and floor. Let all the debris fall on the sheet. When you get to your destination, all you have to do is pull out the sheet, shake it on the ground, and put it back in the car.

- ❧ Color-code your children. Jenny knew that the yellow towels were hers, and Brad knew that his were blue.

- ❧ Make sure that each child has a place to hang clothes and store belongings. This place doesn't have to be expensive. Many times plastic bins and wooden crates work fine.

- ❧ Put the van Gogh artwork of your young artist on the refrigerator, bulletin board, or in a folder designated for that child's age or grade in school. Some of the extra artwork can be used in wrapping grandparents' gifts.

❦ Clean out a bedroom before the arrival of new items. Before birthdays, Christmas, and the change of seasons, go through the bedroom with the child assisting and help clean out old clothes, broken toys, and clothes that are too small. Be sure to use my three-bag system: 1) Give Away, 2) Put Away, and 3) Throw Away. Give obsolete items to friends, neighbors, or charities.

❦ Children need shelves, hooks, and bins. Let the children help decide where these items should be placed in the room.

❦ Each room needs a bulletin board to store all those pictures, awards, certificates, postcards, and special items.

❦ Each child needs to have a study center. Make sure there is plenty of light, basic supplies of pencils, pens, paper, paper clips, a stapler, ruler, hole punch, rubber bands. If this isn't possible, put all these items into a color-coded plastic bin.

❦ At least once a month set aside a special afternoon where the children are invited to the kitchen to prepare a meal or a portion of a meal. Desserts are always a winner. Bring out the aprons and chef's hat—if they dress like cooks, they will really get involved in the process.

❦ I have an old cowbell that is positioned by our kitchen door. Two minutes before a meal I go out and ring that bell very firmly. This is a signal to the members of the family that the food is ready. They have two minutes to get to the table.

❦ Children get bored of doing the same chores all the time. Rotate them periodically.

Helpful Hint:

Rather than nag your children five minutes before they leave for school or an activity, set a small alarm clock to go off five minutes before they are to leave (the oven clock works well, too).

Jobs for Kids

Delegating responsibility to children is such an important aspect of motherhood that you should be giving your children responsibilities at a very young age. Make it fun for them; make games out of it. A three-year-old can dress himself, put his pajamas away, brush his hair, brush his teeth, and make his bed. You can begin to teach your children these things when they're as young as two and three years old. Some more examples: folding clothes, emptying the dishwasher, clearing some of the dishes off the table, emptying wastebaskets, or picking up toys before bedtime (plastic baskets are excellent for toys).

It is our responsibility as parents to train our children and direct them and guide them in the ways that they should go, so that when they become adults they're not domestic invalids. It's important that we give our children responsibilities and train them up. As you go through your home, take your little one with you and begin to show him what you're doing. Often children don't even realize that there's toothpaste on the mirror in the bathroom because they've never been told that they have to wipe it up. They think it just somehow automatically disappears.

Here are some more things children can do:

Three-year-old

1. Get dressed, put pajamas away
2. Brush hair

3. Brush teeth
4. Make bed
5. Fold clothes and small items
6. Empty dishwasher (will need help with this)
7. Clear meal dishes
8. Empty wastebaskets
9. Pick up toys before bed

> *Helpful Hint:*
> Tape pictures of socks, T-shirts, and so forth on dresser drawers in your young children's rooms. They then will know where everything goes when putting their clothes away.

Five-year-old

1. Set table
2. Clean bathroom sink
3. Help clean and straighten drawers and closets
4. Clean up after pet
5. Feed pet
6. Walk dog
7. Dust furniture in room
8. Vacuum room
9. Help put groceries away

Seven-year-old

1. Empty garbage
2. Sweep walks
3. Help in kitchen after dinner
4. Help make lunch for school
5. Do schoolwork
6. Clean out car
7. Iron flat items

Eight-year-old

1. Wash bathroom mirrors

2. Wash windows

3. Wash floors in small area

4. Polish shoes

As your children grow, more responsibility can be given to them:

1. Wash car

2. Mow lawn

3. Make dessert

4. Paint

5. Clean refrigerator

6. Do yard work

7. Iron

8. Fix an entire meal

9. Do grocery shopping

We cannot do it all by ourselves in our homes (when we try, we become frustrated). When we begin to delegate responsibilities to our children and allow them to do some of the work for us, they begin to feel as if they are a vital part of the family.

The Laundry Game

Take a piece of fabric (a remnant or whatever—something with a lot of color in it) and make a laundry bag about 20 inches wide by 36 inches high. You might want to use a king-sized pillowcase with a shoelace strung through the top. Then say to your little ones, "Okay, we're going to play a game." Don't tell them it's work. By the time they're ten, they will realize you've been working them to death, but they don't know it when they're little. Say, "We're going to play a game, and it's called sort-the-laundry." Then get out your laundry bag that has lots of colors and say, "This is the bag where all the dirty clothes that have a lot of colors go. Now find something in this dirty-clothes pile that has a lot of colors." So they run over and pick it up, and you say, "Right! Now put it in the colored laundry bag." So they put it in there.

Then make a bag that is navy blue or dark brown and tell them, "This is where all the dark-colored clothes go." This would be the blue jeans, the brown T-shirts, the navy-blue socks—all those dark-colored clothes. "Now run over and find something that's dark-colored." You see, you're playing a game with them. They do it, and you say, "Great! That's absolutely right!"

Then you make a bag that's all white, and you say, "Now this is where the white dirty clothes go—the white T-shirts, the white socks, the white underwear. They go into the white laundry bag."

Now you're going to give them a little test. You say, "Okay, now find me something that's colored." They run over and pick it up. And then, "Find something that's white." And they put it into the proper bag. What you're doing now is actually teaching children as young as four years old how to sort the laundry.

Bags and More Bags

Another thing I did that really worked out well was to make individual laundry bags for each of the kids to hang in their room behind their door or in their closet. This is where they put their own dirty clothes. Then whoever's job it was for the week to sort the laundry merely went around, collected everybody's laundry bag, and sorted these into three large laundry bags I had by my washing machine.

One gal gave me a great idea, which I think is fantastic if you have the room. Go out and buy three of those plastic trash cans in different colors, and put them in the garage. You can label them white clothes, dark clothes, and colored clothes with a felt-tip pen. Then your kids can sort the clothes by playing a basketball game with the clothes and trying to hit the right containers.

The Chore Basket

Take a good look at the Daily Work Planner Chart. What we would do was to take all the chores for the week, write them on individual pieces of paper, and put them in a basket. Then we would go around one by one and allow the children to choose—to pick out a chore. It was like a little game; whatever they chose was the chore they had to do for the week. And it would go on the Daily Work Planner Chart.

Notice that Mom and Dad are listed on the chart, too. What it shows the kids is that we're working together as a family. At the end of the day, when they've checked their charts and have done their chores as best they can, you can put a little happy face on the chart. Stickers are great also. At the end of the week you can check your chart and say, "You know, our family did a fantastic job this week. We're going to have a picnic at the park (or go bicycling together, or have an evening with popcorn together, or do something else that's fun together) because we've really worked well together in accomplishing this."

Daily Work Planner Chart

Date_____

	Mom	Dad	#1 Child	#2 Child	#3 Child	#4 Child	#5 Child
Sunday							
Monday							
Tuesday							
Wednesday							
Thursday							
Friday							

If you have a wide range of ages in your home, you might want to use two baskets—one for the smaller children and one for the rest of the family. That way the little children don't draw jobs that are too difficult. It is also important that Mom and Dad inspect to make sure the chores are done properly. Remember, "It's not what you expect, but what you inspect" that teaches children to be responsible family members.

Setting the Table

A five-year-old can learn to set the table. It amazed me when our daughter, Jenny, would bring her friends home at 16 or 17 years of age and they didn't even know how to set a table. They didn't know where a knife, fork, and spoon went. It wasn't their fault. It was because Mom or Dad never took the time to teach them. As the five-year-old sets the table you can say, "Okay, Chad, do whatever you want. You can use Mom's good china, or you can use paper plates, or you can have candlelight, or you can put your favorite teddy bear on the table. I don't care—whatever you want to do."

Too many times we put the good china on the table only for when company comes and at Christmas. Who are the most important people in our lives? Our family! And we seldom use the good china for those people who mean the very most to us. I look at it this way: We can't take the china with us, so if a piece gets broken here and there, it gets broken. I would rather have my children be able to enjoy the nicer things and to use them and live with them than to have them in a china cabinet where they can't be enjoyed. So let your children have the freedom to use the good china and teach them as you go along how to set the table.

The Weekly Calendar

You can list those things that are going to go on for the week; you can quickly look through the calendar and see when you're going to be needed, when you're going to need to pick up so-and-so. And you can feel free now because you know where you're needed and where your children will have to be. Check it over and fill it out the night before so you'll know what's happening the next day. Also fill in your work schedule if you work outside your home. Then your family can see it and know what's going on.

Weekly Calendar

	Monday	Tuesday	Wednesday	Thursday	Friday	Saturday	Sunday
Morning							
Noon							
Night							

The Bed Lesson

I asked our son after his second year in college, "Brad, do you make your bed at school?" He replied, "Mom, I'm the only one in my house who makes my bed." I know why he does it, because once when he was about eight years old he hadn't made his bed for four mornings in a row. I had let him get away with it a little now and then, but four mornings was just too much. He was halfway down the block with a couple of his little buddies when I noticed his unmade bed and went running after him. When I caught up with him I said, "Brad, I really hate to do this, but this is the fourth morning in a row you haven't made your bed. So I'm going to have to ask you to please go back in and make your bed." He replied, "Mom, you wouldn't!" I said, "Well, I'm really sorry, but I'm going to have to do it." He responded, "But I'm going to be late for school!" I came back with, "I know you're going to be late for school, but we'll worry about that later." So he came home and made his bed. Then he said, "You know I'm going to need a note for my teacher." I replied, "Fine, I'll be happy to write you a note." I wrote him a note saying that Brad was late because this was the fourth morning in a row that he had not made his bed, and that the teacher could do whatever she wanted with him. You know what? I never had any trouble with Brad making his bed after that!

Helping Kids Come to Breakfast

We get breakfast cooked and call everyone to the table, but they don't come. Isn't that irritating? I think that was one of the things that bothered me the most. How are we going to correct this problem? I said to the children, "We're going to have a meeting." I continued, "You know, I've really got a problem. I call you children for breakfast, but you don't come. Now is there anything you might suggest that could help with this problem?" So they said to me, "Golly, Mom, if you'd just let us know a couple of minutes before breakfast is ready, we'd come right to the table." So that's what we did. You can ring a chime, play the piano, sing a song, blow a whistle—whatever you want to do. Give them a warning to let them know that breakfast or dinner is going to be ready within a few minutes, and they'll come. It absolutely worked beautifully in our family.

Other Helpful Hints

⬝ From a creative mother: After many nights of interrupted sleep, I finally hit on a solution that keeps my five-year-old in her bed—

at least most nights. I labeled one bowl "Mama's Bed Buttons" and another "Christine's Bed Buttons" and put 25 small buttons in each. For every night Christine stays in bed, I owe her one button. She pays me a button if she gets in bed with me. When her button bowl is filled, we do something special—a roller-skating trip, a movie, an outing of her choice. Now she only comes to my bed if she really feels she has to.

ॐ One most-appreciated gift a neighbor gave me after the birth of my first baby was a freshly baked apple pie with a card attached worth eight hours of free babysitting. The pie hit the spot, since I was tired of eating all the hospital food, and it was reassuring to know there was someone available close by to babysit if needed.

ॐ Once a year, have a babysitter swap party. Each attendee must bring the names and telephone numbers of three reliable sitters.

ॐ A tasty variation on the standard peanut-butter-and-jelly sandwich: Make the sandwich as usual, but just before serving, butter the outside of the bread, and brown the sandwich in a hot skillet.

ॐ When sewing buttons on children's clothing, use elastic thread. It makes buttoning much simpler for little fingers.

ॐ Here is a little idea for young children at a fast-food store or restaurant. When you buy the tot a soft drink, cut the straw off short so it is easier to hold and drink. There is less chance of a child spilling or dropping the drink, too.

ॐ Put a plastic cloth under your young child's high chair. After they are finished eating, all you have to do is take the plastic outside and shake off all the crumbs.

Helpful Hint:
To help children remember the proper way to set the table, tell them that fork and left both have four letters, while knife, spoon, and right all have five letters.

Simply Organized...
Meals in Minutes

Quick and Easy Meal Planning

The average woman cooks, plans, markets, chops, prepares, cleans up, or eats out more than 750 meals a year! Doesn't it stand to reason that this is an area where we would need to organize? Feeding our families is certainly a big part of our lives, so here are a few easy steps and hints to make your meal planning successful.

Keep It Simple

Fold an 8 ½" x 11" sheet of paper lengthwise in half. Fold that half crosswise and then in half again to equal eight squares. Write the names of the days of the week in seven of the squares and "Rest" in the eighth square.

Select a main dish for each of the seven squares and plan your meals accordingly. In your planning, consider eating out, company, leftovers, and family favorites. Post your meal planner chart so all family members can see it. Should you be late arriving home, older family members can check the planner and start dinner for you. You can also list on your menu planner which person in the family is to set the table that day or week and who clears off.

Monday Noodle Bake	Tuesday Lentil Rice Casserole
Wednesday Turkey Loaf	Thursday Vegetable Soup
Friday Pizza	Saturday Company
Sunday Chicken Parmesan	Rest

Shopping List

Date_____

Qty.	Staples
____	Cereal
____	Flour
____	Jello
____	Mixes
____	Nuts
____	Stuffing
____	Sugar

Spices
____ Bacon Bits
____ Baking Powder
____ Chocolate
____ Coconut
____ Salt/Pepper
____ Soda

Pasta
____ Inst. Potato
____ Mixes
____ Pasta
____ Rice
____ Spaghetti

Drinks
____ Apple Cider
____ Coffee
____ Juice
____ Sparkling Water
____ Tea

Canned Goods
____ Canned Fruit
____ Canned Meals
____ Canned Meat
____ Canned Veg.
____ Soups

Condiments
____ Ketchup
____ Honey

Qty.
____ Jelly/Jam
____ Mayonnaise
____ Molasses
____ Mustard
____ Oil
____ Peanut Butter
____ Pickles
____ Relish
____ Salad Dressing
____ Shortening
____ Syrup
____ Tomato Paste
____ Tomato Sauce
____ Vinegar

Paper Goods
____ Napkins
____ Paper Towels
____ Plastic Wrap
____ Tissues
____ Toilet Paper
____ Toothpicks
____ Trash Bags
____ Waxed Paper
____ Zip Bags
____ Small
____ Large
____ Paper Plates

Household
____ Bleach
____ Laundry Soap
____ Dish Soap
____ Dishwasher Soap
____ Fabric Softener
____ Furniture Polish
____ Light Bulbs
____ Pet Food
____ Vacuum Bags

Qty.
Fresh Produce
____ Fruit
____ Vegetables

Personal Items
____ Body Soap
____ Deodorant
____ Fem. Protection
____ Hair Care
____ Makeup

Frozen Food
____ Ice Cream
____ Juice
____ TV Dinners
____ Vegetables

Pastry
____ Bread/s
____ Buns
____ Chips
____ Cookies
____ Crackers
____ Croutons

Meat
____ Beef
____ Chicken
____ Pork

Dairy
____ Butter
____ Cheese
____ Cottage Cheese
____ Eggs
____ Milk
____ Sour Cream
____ Yogurt

Work Your Plan

From your menu planner, make out a marketing list. I've created a shopping list where I can simply check off what items I need. List items as they appear on the aisles in your supermarket. This will prevent backtracking and spending more money. A study showed after the first half-hour in the market a woman will spend at least 75 cents per minute! You'll find you will be able to complete your shopping within 30 minutes if you stick to your list.

Shop, if possible, at off hours (early morning, late evening), and shop alone. Both husbands and children can cause compromise on your list. And never shop when you're hungry, because you'll only be tempted to buy junk food.

Beware of supermarket psychology. Higher priced items are stocked at eye level. Food display at the end of aisles may appear to be on sale, but often is not.

And finally, make wise nutritional choices. Instead of ground beef, use ground turkey; darker leaf lettuce instead of light; fresh vegetables in season instead of canned or frozen; whole grain breads instead of white. Study and read labels so you're aware of additives (such as MSG), preservatives, fat content, sodium, etc. Ingredients are listed in descending order by prominence of weight. The first items listed are the main ingredients in the product.

Other Helpful Hints

- ❦ Don't forget Tupper Suppers—premade meals that are stored in Tupperware or containers in the freezer or refrigerator.

- ❦ To speed up baking potatoes, simply put a clean nail through the potato. It will cook in half the time.

❦ Leftover pancakes or waffles? Don't discard them; freeze them. Then pop them into the toaster or oven for a quick and easy breakfast or after-school snack.

❦ Freeze lunchbox sandwiches. They can be made up by the week. Put on all the ingredients except lettuce. It will save time and trouble.

❦ No need to boil those lasagna noodles anymore! Just spread sauce in the bottom of the pan, place hard, uncooked noodles on top and spread sauce on top of noodles. Continue with the other layers, finishing with noodles and sauce. Cover with foil and bake at 350° for 1 hour and 15 minutes.

❦ Before freezing bagels, cut them in half. When you're ready to use them, they will defrost faster and can even be toasted while they are still frozen.

❦ Fruit prepared ahead of time will keep well if you squeeze lemon juice over it and refrigerate. The juice of half a lemon is enough for up to two quarts of cut fruit.

By spending a little time preparing your food and planning your meals, you'll save even more time for the other things you need to do!

Recipes

Sour Cream Cheese Enchiladas

SERVES 4-6

*Our grandson Bevan makes these
for his family at least once a month.*

Ingredients

- 2 bunches green onions
- 1 pint (2 cups) sour cream
- 2 pounds longhorn cheddar cheese, grated
- 3 6-ounce cans enchilada sauce
- 20 8-inch flour tortillas
- butter

Preparation

Preheat oven to 350 degrees. Chop green onions, mix with sour cream. Leave out some onions for top of enchiladas. Warm enchilada sauce in medium saucepan on low. Mix half of the cheddar cheese with sour cream mixture. Butter tortillas and fry until soft, dip in warm sauce and fill with sour cream mixture. Fold enchiladas, place in baking dish, folded side down, and pour remaining sauce over enchiladas. Bake ½ hour at 350 degrees. Put remaining green onions and cheese on top 10 minutes before serving.

Optional
2 cups cooked chicken breasts, cubed

One Pot
Pot Roast

Ingredients
2   10 ½-ounce cans French onion soup
1   10 ½-can beef broth or consommé
1 to 3 pounds of pot roast
1   package baby carrots, about one pound

Preparation
Cut meat into one inch cubes and brown. Put the meat in slow cooker (Crock-Pot); add carrots and rest of the ingredients to it. Cover and cook 6 to 8 hours on low or 4 hours on high. Serve with hot noodles or rice.

Takes 5-7 minutes to prepare!

℃

A man seldom thinks with more earnestness
of anything than he does his dinner.

—SAMUEL JOHNSON

John Wayne's Cheese Casserole

SERVES 6-8

My mama worked for a family who lived next door to John Wayne in Newport Beach, California. They got this recipe from him.

Ingredients

1	pound Monterey Jack cheese, coarsely grated
1	pound cheddar cheese, coarsely grated
2	cans (4 ounce size) green chiles, drained
4	egg whites
4	egg yolks
⅔	cup canned evaporated milk
1	tablespoon flour
½	teaspoon salt
⅛	teaspoon pepper
2	medium tomatoes, sliced

Preparation

Preheat oven to 325 degrees. Remove seeds from chiles and dice. In a large bowl, combine the grated cheese and green chiles. Turn into well-buttered, shallow 2 quart casserole. In large bowl, with electric mixer at high speed, beat egg whites just until stiff peaks form when beater is slowly raised. In a small bowl, combine egg yolks, milk, flour, salt, and pepper; mix until well blended. Using a rubber spatula, gently fold beaten whites into egg-yolk mixture. Pour egg mixture over cheese mixture in casserole, and using a fork, "ooze" it through the cheese. Bake 30 minutes; remove from oven, and arrange sliced tomatoes, overlapping, around edge of casserole. Bake 30 minutes longer, or until a knife inserted in center comes out clean. Garnish with a sprinkling of chopped green chiles, if desired.

Optional
You may use Ortega Green Salsa as a topping with the sliced tomatoes to further enhance this dish.

Southwestern Grilled Chicken

SERVES 8-10

The total California patio meal!

Ingredients
2	medium tomatoes, quartered
2	cups onions, chopped
½	cup red bell pepper, chopped
4	garlic cloves
¼	cup fresh cilantro leaves, packed
⅔	cup soy sauce
6	tablespoons oil
2	tablespoons fresh lime juice
1 ½	teaspoons black pepper

4 to 5 large whole chicken breasts, split, rib bones removed
(boneless breasts can also be used)
parsley, freshly chopped for garnish

Preparation
Place the tomatoes, onions, pepper, garlic, cilantro, soy sauce, oil, lime juice, and black pepper in a blender or food processor and blend for 30 seconds. Pour the marinade over the chicken breasts and marinate, cover and refrigerate, for at least 4 hours,

turning frequently. Remove the chicken from the marinade and grill over medium coals for 20 to 30 minutes, turning frequently and basting with the marinade. Sprinkle the chicken with parsley before serving. Serve with California black beans.

I usually buy 2 cans of black beans and heat and garnish them with cilantro, or you can cook 2 cups black beans and follow the package directions.

Grape-Nut Casserole

We were served this dish in Kosciusko, Mississippi, at the home of our friends Joe and Dean Fenwick with a green salad and rolls.

Ingredients

2	chicken breasts
1	cup water
1	cup vermouth
1 ½	teaspoons salt
½	teaspoon curry
1	10 ½-ounce can mushroom soup
3	tablespoons mayonnaise
1	cup sour cream
½	pound mushrooms
2	boxes Uncle Ben's wild rice
1	cup Grape-Nuts cereal
½	cup butter
1	6-ounce package sliced almonds

Preparation

Combine chicken breasts, water, vermouth, salt, and curry, cook till tender. Debone chicken and soak in broth overnight.

Strain broth and cook wild rice in broth, add water if needed. Sauté mushrooms in 1 tablespoon butter. Combine mushroom soup, mayonnaise, and sour cream with sautéed mushrooms. Cook at 350 degrees till bubbly. For topping, sauté Grape-Nuts, butter, and almonds. Put over chicken, brown in oven.

Napa Valley Cheese Soup

SERVES 6

We serve this on a cold winter's day with crunchy bread and Caesar salad, and we always get compliments!

Ingredients

1	cup potatoes, diced (optional)
4 ½	cups chicken stock
½	cup carrots, diced
½	cup celery, diced
½	cup zucchini, diced
2	tablespoons butter
2	tablespoons onion, finely chopped
½	cup flour
1	cup sharp cheddar cheese, gated
¼	cup Parmesan cheese, grated
10	drops hot sauce
¼	teaspoon white pepper
½	cup dry white wine
1 ½	cups whipping cream
	salt to taste
	parsley, freshly chopped

Preparation

In 2 quart saucepan add 1 ½ cups broth to carrots, potatoes, celery, and zucchini. Bring to a boil and simmer for 10 minutes. In 4-5 quart saucepan melt butter and add onion, sauté until transparent. Blend in flour and cook 5 to 7 minutes. Stirring constantly, be careful not to brown. Stir in remaining broth, slowly whisk over low heat until thickened. Add both cheeses and stir until melted. Season with hot sauce, salt, pepper, and wine. Stir in cream and serve; salt to taste and garnish with chopped parsley.

Meal Planning Made Easy

The average homemaker plans, shops, chops, pares, cooks, and cleans up for more than 750 meals a year! Keeping our families fed is a major part of our lives.

A few years ago, I found myself often serving as a short-order cook, trying to please everyone in the family. At any one breakfast I might fix French toast, waffles, scrambled eggs, pancakes, bacon, sausage, fruit, cold cereal, and oatmeal. By the time breakfast was over, I was ready to climb back into bed! Something needed to change before I lost my sanity.

I came upon a relatively simple solution: I decided to plan a week's worth of breakfasts, incorporating each family member's favorite breakfast one morning each week. On Monday, I might fix my son Brad's favorite, French toast; on Tuesday my husband Bob's favorite, fried eggs over medium. I keep Sunday open for the cook's choice (or I let my husband cook that morning!).

It became such a pleasure to fix breakfast with this system that I very quickly expanded my planning to all our meals. And it motivated me to begin looking for new and interesting recipes and to scour the newspapers for money-saving sales. Now I always plan my meals an entire week ahead, check my cupboards and pantry to see what I have on hand, and make a marketing list for my trip to the grocery store. It saves me time and money.

Brother Ed's
Fettucine with Zucchini and Mushrooms

SERVES 6

My brother is a great cook!
He takes after our father the chef.

Ingredients

1	16-ounce package of fettucine noodles (I use spinach noodles if I can find them)
½	pound mushrooms, sliced
¾	cup butter
1 ¼	pounds zucchini, cut into julienne strips
1	cup heavy cream
¾	cup Parmesan cheese, freshly grated
½	cup parsley

Preparation

In a large skillet sauté mushrooms in ¼ cup butter over medium heat. Add zucchini. Add cream and ½ cup butter; cut into pieces. Bring the liquid to a boil and simmer for 3 minutes. Cook noodles, drain and add to the skillet with fresh Parmesan cheese. Add parsley and toss with a wooden fork, gently combining mixture well. Transfer to a heated platter or large pasta bowl. Serve with additional fresh Parmesan cheese.

Roast
Pork Loin

SERVES 6-8

A great company meal—our guests always love it.

Ingredients
2   teaspoons olive oil
1   tablespoon black pepper
1   teaspoon nutmeg
1   teaspoon cinnamon
3 to 4 pound boneless pork loin roast

Preparation
Blend oil, pepper, nutmeg, and cinnamon in small bowl. Rub mixture onto pork; cover completely. Place pork in shallow pan; roast in 350 degree oven for 1 to 1 ½ hours or until internal temperature is 155 degrees. Remove pork from oven; let stand 10 minutes before slicing.

Serve with rice, vegetables, and pineapple rings with cottage cheese on a bed of lettuce.

℃

Hunger is the first course of a good dinner.
—FRENCH PROVERB

Salmon Fettucine

SERVES 4

Ingredients
- 1   small leek
- 1   small zucchini
- 1   tablespoon olive oil
-     salt and pepper
- 8   ounces heavy cream
- 3   ounces feta cheese
- 1   pound fettucine
- 4 to 6 ounces smoked salmon, thinly sliced
-     parsley, freshly chopped

Preparation

Dice the leek and zucchini and sauté in a frying pan with olive oil until golden brown. Add a bit of salt and pepper. Stir in cream and feta cheese, reduce sauce to the consistency you like. Cook the pasta as suggested on the package, drain. Stir into the saucepan, then serve. Top with smoked salmon (rolled) and garnish with fresh parsley.

Serve with Caesar salad and Italian bread.

The Pasta Queen's Nicoise

SERVES 4-6

I go to Maria, the "Pasta Queen,"
anytime I need pasta advice.
This is a favorite she made for us.

Ingredients

6	large, ripe tomatoes, seeded and chopped
4	cloves garlic, peeled and finely chopped
½	cup capers, drained and rinsed
1 ½	cups black olives, pitted
⅓	cup loosely packed, fresh oregano leaves, plus more for garnish
¼	cup flat leaf parsley leaves, torn
3	tablespoons extra-virgin olive oil
	dash of balsamic vinegar
1	teaspoon salt
1	teaspoon freshly ground pepper
1	pound dry pasta, such as rigatoni, penne, rigate, or orecchiette
1	12-ounce can white tuna, drained well

Preparation

In a large bowl, combine all ingredients except pasta and tuna. Stir well, cover, and let sit for 1 hour. Set aside about 1 ½ cups. Cook pasta in boiling salted water until *al dente*. Drain well. Add to large bowl of sauce along with tuna, and combine. Serve in shallow bowls topped with some of the reserved sauce. Garnish with oregano.

Optional

Leftover grilled tuna or swordfish makes a delicious substitute for the canned tuna.

Barnes' Summer Salad

SERVES 6-8

A Meal in One

Bob Hawkins, retired C.E.O. of Harvest House Publishers, requests this meal every time he comes to dinner in our house.

Ingredients

All chopped:

1 to 2 heads romaine lettuce

2   large tomatoes

4   hard boiled eggs

4   cooked chicken breasts, cubed

1   pound bacon, cooked and crumbled

1   bunch green onions, chopped

1   cup blue cheese, crumbled

1   package mild Italian Good Seasons dressing mix made according to directions

1   16-ounce bottle ranch or blue cheese dressing

Preparation

Mix lettuce, tomatoes, eggs, chicken, bacon, onions, and cheese in large bowl. Toss with half of the Italian and half of the ranch dressing. Don't overload—just add enough to cover well.

Chili
The Low-Fat Way

SERVES 6-8

This is a zesty chili I serve on a chilly winter's day.
It hits the spot with hot buttered tortillas.

Ingredients

1　medium onion, chopped

¼　cup green pepper, chopped

4　cups water, divided

1　15- to 16-ounce can great northern beans, rinsed
　　　and drained

1　6-ounce can salt-free tomato paste

1　14 ½-ounce can low-salt diced tomatoes, undrained

2 to 4 teaspoons chili powder

1　teaspoon salt, optional

½　teaspoon pepper

Preparation

In a large saucepan, cook the onion and green pepper in ½ cup water until tender. Add beans, tomato paste, and tomatoes. Stir in chili powder, salt if desired, pepper, and remaining water; bring to a boil. Reduce heat, cover, and simmer for 20 minutes.

Foolproof Rib Roast

Yes, it does work. I do it often—well, three times a year!

Ingredients
1 standing rib roast, 4 pounds or more (depending on how many servings you need)

Preparation
Bring beef to room temperature. Place rib side down, on rack, in shallow roasting pan. Roast for 1 hour at 375 degrees. Turn off oven, but do not open door; leave roast in oven. Approximately an hour before dinner, turn oven on to 375 degrees and roast 30 minutes to an hour longer, depending on size of roast and degree of doneness desired (30 minutes for medium rare). Remove to hot platter and let stand 15 minutes before carving.

Tip
Start roast around 11:00 A.M. for dinner. For roast of more than 10 pounds, the final roasting time should be increased 1 hour. Use meat thermometer to check degree of doneness, as oven temperatures and room temperature of the meat can make a difference. 140 degrees = rare, 160 degrees = medium, and 170 degrees = well done. Serve with steamed new potatoes, green beans, French bread, and crisp green salad.

❦

Laughter is brightest where food is best.

—IRISH PROVERB

Your Kitchen Essentials

No matter how large or small your kitchen is, you can tailor it to suit your style, if you give some thought to your cooking habits and needs. Start by taking inventory. Here are what I consider the essentials for every kitchen.

Pans

1	10" skillet with lid
1	8" to 10" omelet pan
1	roasting pan
2	bread pans
2	cookie sheets
1	double boiler
1	Dutch oven or similar type of pan
1	set of covered casserole dishes

Basic Utensils

	Start with a good set of knives and include a steel sharpener to keep your knives properly maintained.
	a variety of wooden spoons
1	set of measuring cups
1	mallet (for tenderizing less expensive cuts of meat)
1	spatula
	shears (great for cutting parsley, green onions, and meat)
1	rolling pin
	storage bowls
1	vegetable cleaner
1	cheese slicer
	tongs
1	garlic press

Gadgets

	grater
	colander

sifter
vegetable steamer
food grinder
eggbeater
whisk
egg slicer

Optional Larger Equipment
mixer
toaster oven
blender
food processor
wheat mill
microwave oven
an extra freezer

California Swiss Steak

Ingredients
1   package onion soup mix
1   cup water
1   cup wine
1   10 ½-ounce can mushroom soup
2 to 3 pounds Swiss steak, browned in a Dutch oven

Preparation
Combine onion soup mix, water, wine, and mushroom soup. Pour over browned steak. Bake covered for 1 hour at 350 degrees, then uncover and bake 15 minutes more.

Otto's Brisket

This was my father's brisket recipe.
He was a master chef trained in Europe.

Ingredients

1	2 to 4 pound brisket of beef
1	can beer
1	onion, quartered
3	garlic cloves, chopped
3	carrots, sliced
2	tablespoons sour cream
1 ½	teaspoons Dijon mustard
2	teaspoons horseradish

Preparation

Put brisket in glass dish or oven pan. Add half of the beer, cover and cook 1 hour at 400 degrees. Add the other half of the beer, onion, garlic cloves, and carrots. Cover and continue to cook at 325 degrees 3 to 4 hours.

To make gravy, add to juices sour cream, Dijon mustard, and horseradish.

Serve with sliced tomatoes and cucumbers sprinkled with red wine vinegar and olive oil; biscuits or corn bread; and/or roasted red potatoes.

Chad's
Shrimp & Spaghetti

SERVES 6

Our grandson, Chad, loves shrimp.
He cooks this for all of us.

Ingredients

3   tablespoons extra-virgin olive oil
2   cloves fresh garlic, pressed
1   small onion, chopped
1   pound shrimp (prawns), peeled
⅓   cup dry white cooking wine
10   ounces ripe plum Roma tomatoes (egg shaped), peeled
         and chopped (or canned plum tomatoes, drained
         and chopped)
     salt and freshly ground pepper
1   pound spaghetti
1   tablespoon chopped fresh flat leaf parsley (Italian
         parsley)

Preparation

In a large pot, bring 5 quarts salted water to a boil. In a large frying pan, heat olive oil over low heat, sauté garlic and onion until translucent, stirring frequently, about 3 minutes. Add shrimp, raise heat to medium, and cook, stirring constantly for 2 minutes. Add the wine and continue cooking until it evaporates, about 2 minutes. Add tomatoes and season to taste with salt and pepper. Cook for 2 more minutes.

Add spaghetti to the boiling water and cook until tender.

Drain pasta and transfer it to the frying pan containing the tomato sauce. Add the parsley and cook over medium heat, stirring frequently, for 2 minutes.

Arrange the pasta on a warm platter and serve piping hot.

Serve with a fresh green salad, tossed with Italian dressing and garlic toast.

Sue's Sensational Parmesan Chicken

SERVES 6

Ingredients

1	cup soft bread crumbs
½	cup Parmesan cheese
¼	cup minced parsley
⅛	teaspoon salt
⅛	teaspoon garlic powder
½	cup butter, melted
2	pounds skinless, boneless chicken breasts
	paprika

Preparation

Mix bread crumbs, Parmesan cheese, parsley, salt, and garlic powder. Place butter in 9" x 13" dish. Coat chicken with butter, then dip both sides of chicken in crumb mixture, layer in pan with rest of butter.

Garnish with paprika. Bake at 350 degrees for 1 hour. Baste twice during baking. Cover with foil if chicken browns too much before it's done.

Serve with brown rice, steamed broccoli, asparagus or green beans, and sliced tomatoes.

California Chili Casserole

SERVES 4

Ingredients

1	3-ounce package cream cheese, at room temperature
¾	cup cottage cheese
½	cup sour cream
3	tablespoons green onion, minced
2	tablespoons green chiles, diced
¼	teaspoon salt
1	8-ounce can chili and beans
2	4-ounce cans ripe olives, sliced
2	cups corn chips
½	cup sharp cheddar cheese, grated

Preparation

Preheat oven to 350 degrees. Blend cream cheese until smooth; add cottage cheese, sour cream, onion, green chiles, and salt; mix well. In a separate bowl, combine chili and beans with olives. Layer in buttered 1 ½ quart casserole dish, in order, 1 cup corn chips, cheese mixture, 1 cup corn chips, chili-olive mixture. Sprinkle top with more crushed chips.

Bake for 25 minutes. Remove from oven; sprinkle with cheese and bake 5 to 8 minutes longer or until cheese is melted.

You Won't Say
Yuck, Because It's Yummy Tuna Casserole

SERVES 4-6

Ingredients

2   eggs

2   cups (1 pint) cottage cheese (You may use low-fat cottage cheese, if preferred)

1   6 ½-ounce can light tuna, drained and flaked

⅛   teaspoon pepper

½   teaspoon Worcestershire sauce

1   6-ounce bag of crushed potato chips (Lay's or Ruffles work well)

Preparation

Prepare water bath by placing large shallow pan of water in center of oven; preheat to 375 degrees. (Water should be deep enough to come halfway up side of 1 quart casserole.)

Beat eggs in large bowl, blend in cottage cheese, tuna, and remaining ingredients except chips. Pour into buttered 1 quart casserole and sprinkle with chips. Set in water bath and bake 35 minutes or until just set.

Planning the Perfect Kitchen

The key rule in organizing your kitchen is, "Things that work together are stored together." Take a few minutes to think through your daily work pattern and plan your space accordingly. For example, if you do a lot of baking, set up a baking center. It might be a countertop or a convenient cupboard or even a mobile worktable that can be rolled into your kitchen on baking day. Your mixer, baking pans, utensils, and canisters should all be readily accessible to this center.

Items seldom used, such as a turkey platter, deviled egg dish, roasting pan, seasonal tableware, and picnic gear, should be kept on higher shelves or stored in the garage on a special, easily accessible shelf. That will free space in your kitchen for the regularly used items.

Looking for some more ideas?

- Spices can be found quickly if stored in alphabetical order on a lazy Susan or a wooden spice rack on your wall.

- Use a crock to store utensils such as wooden spoons, whisks, meat mallet, ladles, and spatula on the stove. This can free up a drawer and allows for quick retrieval.

- If you get a new set of flatware, keep the old set to loan out when friends have buffets or church socials, or for family camping trips.

Once you've planned and organized your kitchen, you'll be amazed how much time you save and how much smoother mealtime preparation goes. And always be on the lookout for new and more efficient ways to store your equipment and food.

All-in-One Meal

SERVES 8-10

Ingredients

2	teaspoons salt
½	teaspoon pepper
1	teaspoon paprika
2	medium potatoes
1	cup celery
4	medium carrots
1	large green pepper
3	medium onions
2	pounds ground beef or ground turkey
1 ½	cups cottage cheese (You may use low-fat cottage cheese, if preferred)
1	16-ounce can stewed tomatoes

Preparation

Combine the seasonings; set aside. Peel and thinly slice potatoes; chop celery and carrots; mince green pepper; chop or slice and ring onions. Set all aside. Chunk hamburger into frying pan and brown. Drain excess fat and blend in cottage cheese.

In buttered 4 quart Dutch oven, layer the following in order; sprinkling seasonings over each: potatoes, celery and carrots, hamburger mixture, green pepper and onion; top with tomatoes and juice. Cover and bake at 350 degrees for 1 ½ hours. Uncover for last half hour.

Serve in individual soup bowls.

Fried Chicken with Garlic

SERVES 4

My dad, the chef, used lots of garlic in his recipes.

Ingredients
Marinade:

1	cup sour cream
2	cloves garlic, crushed
1	tablespoon lemon juice
1	teaspoon Worcestershire sauce
1 ½	teaspoons seasoned salt
¼	teaspoon pepper
1	2 ½ pound frying chicken
	flour and cooking oil

Preparation
Blend marinade ingredients in medium bowl.

Cut chicken into serving pieces. Dip pieces in marinade to coat; put in glass dish, spoon on remaining marinade, cover and refrigerate overnight.

Dredge marinated chicken pieces in flour and fry in hot cooking oil, 1 inch deep, until browned and crisp on both sides. Reduce heat and fry slowly until tender, about 40 minutes total. Do not crowd chicken in pan and do not cover.

This is home fried chicken at its best. And it's great with squash, biscuits, and mashed potatoes.

Chile Rellenos

SERVES 8

Ingredients

1	7-ounce can whole green chiles
½	pound Monterey Jack cheese, grated
½	pound cheddar cheese, grated
3	eggs
1	cup biscuit mix
3	cups milk
	seasoned salt

Preparation

Preheat your oven to 325 degrees.

Split the chiles, then rinse and remove seeds. Dry on a paper towel and arrange on the bottom of an 8 ½" x 11" baking dish. Sprinkle the grated cheeses evenly over the top of the chiles. Beat the eggs, then add the biscuit mix and milk and blend well.

Pour batter over the cheese and chile layer. Sprinkle with seasoned salt and bake for 50 to 55 minutes, until golden brown.

Serve hot. Top with salsa for extra zing. For extra protein, add shredded, cooked chicken after the chili layer. Spanish rice and beans go great with this meal. You can top the beans and rice with some Monterey Jack and cheddar cheese.

Emilie's
Orange Chicken

SERVES 4

Ingredients

½ cup butter
½ cup red currant jelly
¼ cup Worcestershire sauce
2 large cloves garlic, crushed
1 tablespoon Dijon mustard
1 teaspoon powdered ginger
3 dashes Tabasco sauce
8 skinless chicken breast pieces
        or 1 whole chicken, skinned and quartered

Preparation

Combine butter, jelly, Worcestershire sauce, garlic, mustard, ginger, and Tabasco. Cook over medium/low heat till smooth. Cool sauce. Place skinned and quartered chicken in baking pan (or 8 skinless chicken breast pieces).

Pour sauce over all; marinate in refrigerator for 2 to 3 hours, covered.

Preheat oven to 350 degrees.

Cover chicken and bake for 1 hour. Uncover; increase temperature to 400 degrees and continue to bake, basting frequently until chicken is an even dark brown.

Serve with rice pilaf and steamed zucchini.

Aunt Lisa's Chicken

This dish comes from Terra Torelli. It's simple and delicious!

Ingredients

- 4 skinless chicken breasts
- 1 ½ sticks of butter (¾ cup), cold
  salt
  pepper
  Schilling's onion powder
- 1 whole onion
- 1 green bell pepper
- 3 of your favorite kinds of cheeses, grated
  (approximately 2 cups of cheese)

Preparation

Preheat oven to 350 degrees.

Clean the chicken, then sprinkle with salt, pepper, and onion powder. (Do not overcoat with the seasonings.) After the chicken is seasoned, place it in a glass dish. Take 1 ¼ sticks of cold butter and cut it into chunks. Place the butter all around and on top of the seasoned chicken. Cover the dish with foil and bake for 1 hour.

While you are waiting for the chicken, chop the onion and bell pepper into small chunk pieces. Place the chopped pieces into a small skillet with remaining ¼ stick of butter and sauté until limp. Spoon over cooked chicken and sprinkle with cheese. Place in the oven until cheese melts, approximately 5 minutes.

This dinner is great served with baked potatoes, fresh green beans, and a nice green salad.

Chicken Cashew

SERVES 4-6

Ingredients

- 4   chicken breasts
- ½   cup flour
- 1   teaspoon salt
- 1   teaspoon pepper
- ⅓   cup olive oil

Sauce

- 1   13-ounce can pineapple chunks, in heavy syrup
- 1   cup sugar
- 2   tablespoons cornstarch
- ¾   cup cider vinegar
- 1   tablespoon soy sauce
- ¼   teaspoon ginger powder
- 1   chicken bouillon cube
- 1   large green pepper, very thinly sliced
- ¾   cup cashews

Preparation

Skin and bone the chicken, then cut into strips. Combine flour, salt, and pepper; coat chicken. Brown chicken in oil in a large skillet or wok. Place in a large baking dish and set aside. To make the sauce, drain the pineapple and reserve the juice. Add enough water to the juice to make 1 ½ cups liquid. In a saucepan, combine sugar, cornstarch, pineapple liquid, vinegar, soy sauce, ginger, and bouillon. Bring to a boil and cook for 2 minutes over medium heat, stirring constantly. Pour the sauce over the chicken and bake uncovered for 30 minutes in a 350 degree oven. Top with the pineapple, green pepper, and cashews and bake another 30 minutes. Serve over rice.

Em's
Meat Loaf

Ingredients

1 ½   pounds lean ground beef or ground turkey
1   egg
½   cup onion, chopped
1   tablespoon chopped or pressed garlic, fresh
½   cup green pepper, chopped
¾   cup celery, finely chopped
¾   cup oatmeal
¾   cup low-fat milk or non-fat milk
½   cup ketchup
1   teaspoon dry mustard
    salt and pepper to taste
¼   cup wheat germ

Preparation

Combine all except wheat germ and shape into a loaf. Roll in wheat germ and bake 1 hour at 325 degrees.

I don't put my loaf in a loaf pan. I use a Pyrex dish. Sometimes I'll make 4 smaller loaves for individual servings. That way you don't have to slice, and they brown on all sides. Serve with baked potatoes and a vegetable.

Ground Turkey Noodle Bake

SERVES 6-8

This casserole will be a family and potluck supper favorite.

Ingredients

1	8-ounce package medium or wide egg noodles
1	tablespoon butter or oil
1	pound ground turkey
2	8-ounce cans tomato sauce
1	8-ounce package cream cheese, at room temperature
1	cup cottage cheese
¼	cup sour cream or low-fat sour cream
⅓	cup green onion, minced
1	tablespoon green pepper, minced

Preparation

Cook noodles according to package directions, add 1 tablespoon butter (or oil) to water; drain. Brown turkey in large frying pan, break into small pieces. Drain excess fat. Stir in tomato sauce and remove from heat. Blend cream cheese to smooth; blend in cottage cheese, sour cream, onion, and green pepper. Spread half the noodles over bottom of buttered 9" x 13" baking dish; cover with cheese mixture and then remaining noodles. Top with meat sauce. Bake at 350 degrees 20 to 25 minutes.

Hamburger Noodles Italiano

Sauté 1 clove crushed garlic with turkey. Add 1 teaspoon chili powder, ½ teaspoon basil, ½ teaspoon leaf oregano, and a pinch of ground cloves to meat sauce. Serve with shredded Parmesan cheese.

A Little Preparation

Preparing food as soon as it's brought home from the grocery store is a tremendous time-saver. No, I don't mean cook the food—just prepare it.

- ❦ If you already know how you will use your vegetables, they can be cleaned, cut or chopped, placed in plastic bags or Tupperware containers, and stored in the refrigerator—ready for salads, steamed vegetables, soups, or casseroles.

- ❦ Onions and green peppers can be chopped, placed in an airtight container or plastic bag, and frozen.

- ❦ A large block of cheese can be grated and frozen, allowing you to remove a portion whenever needed.

- ❦ Salad greens can be cleaned, drained, and stored for the week's salad. Remove the water from greens by putting them in a lingerie bag and placing them in the washing machine on the "spin" cycle for about two minutes. The greens will stay fresh and crisp for up to two weeks when stored in a plastic bag or plastic container in the refrigerator.

- ❦ Fruit prepared ahead of time will keep well if you squeeze lemon juice over it, toss, and refrigerate. The juice of half a lemon is enough for up to two quarts of cut fruit.

- ❦ Boil several eggs at once. They'll keep!

- ❦ Fry up ground beef and put into Tupperware. Freeze and it's ready for any dish.

- ❦ Fry the whole pound of bacon ahead and take what you need for salads, B.L.T.s, etc.

Tortilla Chip Casserole

SERVES 6-8

Kids love these flavors!

Ingredients

1	medium onion, finely chopped
2	tablespoons butter
2	8-ounce cans tomato sauce
1	4-ounce can green chiles, diced
2	teaspoons oregano
1	teaspoon salt
1	8-ounce package tortilla chips
½	pound Monterey Jack cheese, cut in ½-inch cubes
2 to 3	cups chunked, cooked chicken, skinned and boned
1	cup sour cream at room temperature
⅓	cup cheddar cheese, grated

Preparation

Sauté onion in butter until transparent. Add tomato sauce, chiles, oregano, and salt. Simmer, uncovered, for 10 minutes; remove from heat. Layer in buttered 2 ½ to 3 quart casserole, in order, half the following: tortilla chips, Jack cheese, chicken, and sauce. Repeat with remaining half of ingredients. Bake at 325 degrees 20 minutes. Remove from oven and spread sour cream over top; wreath with grated cheddar. Broil just until cheese melts. Serve immediately.

Gourmet
Fillet of Sole

SERVES 6

A party touch for fish fillets.
A handsome buffet all-in-one main dish.

Ingredients

1	6-ounce package white and wild rice mix
1	10-ounce package frozen asparagus spears or 1½ pounds fresh asparagus
1	cup celery, finely chopped
3	tablespoons butter
3	tablespoons flour
1	cup milk
½	teaspoon salt
1	teaspoon Worcestershire sauce
1	tablespoon fresh lemon juice
1	cup sour cream, at room temperature
½	teaspoon hot sauce
6	sole fillets (1½ to 2 pounds)
½	fresh lemon
2	tablespoons Parmesan cheese
2	tablespoons sliced almonds, lightly toasted

Preparation

Cook rice according to package directions, spoon into buttered 8½" x 11" baking dish. Cook asparagus according to package directions; drain. Meanwhile, sauté celery in butter. Stir in flour and cook 1 minute; add milk all at once and cook, stirring, until sauce thickens. Add salt, Worcestershire sauce, and lemon juice. Empty sour cream into medium bowl, gradually add hot sauce, stirring constantly. Sprinkle fillets lightly with juice of half a lemon; salt to taste. Roll each fish fillet around 2 or 3 asparagus spears; arrange roll-ups on top of rice, lapped edge down. Spoon sour cream sauce over fish, sprinkle with cheese and almonds. Bake at 350 degrees for 25 minutes or just until fish becomes milky white and flakes easily.

Quick Burger Stroganoff

SERVES 4

Ingredients

1	medium onion, chopped
2	tablespoons cooking oil
1	pound lean ground beef or ground turkey
1	10 ½-ounce can cream of mushroom soup (You may use low-fat)
2	tablespoons ketchup or chili sauce
1	small can sliced mushrooms, drained
1	cup sour cream, at room temperature
	salt

Preparation

Sauté onion in oil until transparent; add beef and cook until browned. Drain excess fat. Blend in soup, ketchup, and sliced mushrooms; heat through. Remove from heat; add sour cream all at once and blend well. Heat gently to serving temperature. Salt to taste. Serve over hot noodles or rice. Four ounces of dry noodles makes 2 to 3 hearty or 4 moderate servings.

Garlic
Salmon Bake

Ingredients

1   pound salmon fillet
¼   cup olive oil
5   cloves garlic, chopped
¼   cup fresh parsley, minced
1   teaspoon dried basil
½   teaspoon salt
½   teaspoon pepper

Preparation

Spread olive oil over salmon in baking dish. Chop enough garlic to cover top of salmon. Put the fresh parsley over salmon and sprinkle with the spices. Bake at 350 degrees for 15 to 20 minutes, until salmon flakes easily.

Serve with fresh or frozen asparagus and buttered pasta sprinkled lightly with grated Parmesan cheese.

*"Me is hungry," announced Teddy, who began to think that
with so much cooking going on it was about time
for somebody to eat something.*

—LOUISA MAY ALCOTT
Little Women

Boboli Pizza
Shrimp Style

SERVES 8

Seafood cocktail sauce adds a different taste to a traditional food.
This is also good as an hors d'oeuvre.

Ingredients

1	16-ounce Boboli Italian bread shell
½	cup seafood cocktail sauce
4	ounces low-fat cheese (mozzarella or cheddar)
2	cups cooked shrimp
	thinly sliced green pepper, onions, mushrooms, and tomatoes

Preparation

Preheat oven to 450 degrees. Place Boboli on pizza pan. Spoon on the cocktail sauce and add cheese. Arrange shrimp and vegetables over cheese. Bake for 8 to 10 minutes or until cheese is melted.

Yoli's Budget Chicken Dinner

SERVES 4-6

Ingredients

- 1   10 ½-ounce can cream of celery soup
- 1   cup white wine
- ½   package Lipton Onion Soup Mix
- 2   bay leaves
- 6   chicken breasts (skinless, boneless—optional)

Preparation

Mix soup, wine, onion soup mix, and bay leaves. Pour mixture over chicken breasts and bake 1 hour at 350 degrees. Serve over white rice. Garnish with sliced almonds. Herb Biscuits (next page) are great with this.

C

Sit down and feed, and welcome to our table.

—SHAKESPEARE

Herb Biscuits

Ingredients

1   package Pillsbury biscuits
1   stick butter, melted
½   teaspoon thyme
½   teaspoon sage
½   teaspoon garlic powder

Preparation

Cut each biscuit in quarters with scissors. Combine butter, thyme, sage, and garlic powder.

Dip each quarter in butter mixture. Place on cookie sheet.

Bake at 300 degrees until brown, about 12 to 20 minutes.

ℭ

*Part of the secret of success is to eat what
you like and let the food fight it out inside.*

—Mark Twain

Timesaving Tips

Use the time when you're watching television for jobs like shelling nuts. Children often like to help in this task, especially if they can nibble while they help.

Learn to do two things at once when working in the kitchen. I highly recommend a cordless phone (or a long extension cord) so you can reach every corner of the kitchen. While you're on the phone, you can…

- *load or unload the dishwasher*
- *clean the refrigerator*
- *cook a meal*
- *mop the floor*
- *clean under the kitchen sink*

Store food in a single layer to allow proper air circulation and to speed the freezing process.

Before freezing fresh bagels, cut them in half. When you're ready to use them, they will defrost faster and can even be toasted while they are still frozen.

Make up your shopping list according to your market. Go aisle by aisle so you don't have to backtrack.

Don't shop when you're hungry. You'll fill your pantry with foods you don't have a clue what to do with.

Stuffed Pork Chops a la Yoli

SERVES 4

Can't think of what to serve...this is it!
I've served this to everyone.

Ingredients
4   thick pork chops, have butcher slice with a pocket

Stuffing
2   cups cheddar cheese, grated
2   apples, chopped
2   cups bread crumbs
1   teaspoon cinnamon
1   cup orange juice
1   cup golden raisins

Sauce
2   cups maple syrup
1   cup white wine
⅓   cup grated fresh ginger
⅓   cup soy sauce
½   cup flax seed oil

Preparation
Soak stuffing ingredients with orange juice. Mix and stuff into chops, close opening with toothpicks. Put into a square dish. Blend all sauce ingredients and pour over chops. Bake at 350 degrees, covered with foil for ½ hour and then uncovered for ½ hour. Serve with wild rice and baked tomatoes sprinkled with garlic powder and Parmesan cheese.

Quickie
Spoon Bread

Our grandson, Chad, loves making spoon bread and asks to do it often. He began making this recipe when he was nine years old.

Ingredients

1   box Jiffy corn bread mix
2   cups creamed corn
1   small can green chiles, chopped
1   teaspoon sugar
1   egg

Preparation

Mix well and spoon into muffin pan lined with cupcake papers. Bake according to package directions.

The flickering of the blaze showed
preparations for a cozy dinner.

—CHARLES DICKENS

Lemon Baked Salmon

SERVES 4

Good for any fat fish such as bluefish, herring, mackerel, pompano, whitefish, salmon, or mullet.

Ingredients

2   pounds salmon steaks
1   tablespoon butter, unsalted
     juice of ½ to 1 lemon
⅛   teaspoon salt (optional)
     paprika
     fresh minced or dried parsley flakes

Preparation

Place baking pan in oven with butter to melt. Lay steaks evenly in pan in melted butter and top with lemon juice, salt, paprika, and parsley. Bake uncovered at 350 degrees for 20 to 30 minutes, basting 1 or 2 times. Serve with tartar sauce.

Tartar Sauce

Blend thoroughly with wire whisk:

⅓   cup plain nonfat yogurt
1   tablespoon mayonnaise
1   tablespoon sweet pickle relish
1 ½   teaspoons lemon juice
½   teaspoon prepared mustard
⅛   teaspoon dill weed
⅛   teaspoon garlic powder

Sweet and Sour Beans

*Absolutely yummy, easy to prepare,
and takes freezing especially well.*

Ingredients

1	pound ground turkey
½	teaspoon nutmeg
½	teaspoon sage
½	teaspoon thyme leaves
¹⁄₁₆	teaspoon cayenne pepper
2	medium onions, sliced and separated into rings
⅓	cup apple cider vinegar
¼	cup honey
1	teaspoon prepared mustard
1	teaspoon salt
2	15-ounce cans butter beans, drained and rinsed
2	15 ¼-ounce cans green lima beans, drained and rinsed
2	15 ¼-ounce cans red kidney beans, drained and rinsed
2	16-ounce cans vegetarian beans in tomato sauce (Heinz)
½	teaspoon garlic powder

Preparation

Blend turkey with seasonings and brown, remove from pan. Add onions to the pan with a little water and cook covered until tender, but not browned; drain off excess water. Add vinegar, honey, mustard, and salt; simmer covered for 20 minutes. In large bowl, combine onion mixture and turkey with the beans and garlic powder.

Optional

Blend together and stir in, to taste:

¼   cup molasses

¼   cup ketchup

1   teaspoon Worcestershire sauce

Favorite Tamale Pie

SERVES 6

As a young bride I was asked to bring tamale pie to a potluck for Bob's staff at school. I had never made nor tasted a tamale pie in my life! Forty-eight years later I'm still making it.

Ingredients

1   pound ground turkey or beef

1   small onion, chopped

1   small green pepper, chopped

⅛   teaspoon garlic powder, or 1 clove garlic, minced

2   cups tomato, spaghetti, or pasta sauce

10   ounces frozen corn

2   4-ounce cans sliced ripe olives, drained

1 ½   teaspoons chili powder

½   teaspoon salt

1   cup cold water

1   cup cornmeal

1   cup water

1   tablespoon butter

½   teaspoon salt

Preparation

Brown together turkey, onion, green pepper, and garlic in large frying pan. Stir in sauce, corn, olives, chili powder, and salt. Simmer briefly and pour into 2 quart baking pan.

Make cornmeal topping. Whisk cold water and cornmeal together until smooth in small mixing bowl; set aside. Place remaining cup of water, butter, and ½ teaspoon salt in saucepan and bring to boil. Whisk cornmeal mixture into boiling water; cook and stir over moderately low heat until thickened, about 2 minutes. Topping should not be runny.

Spread hot cornmeal topping evenly and completely to the edges over top of pie filling. Bake uncovered at 350 degrees about 50 to 60 minutes or until crust is done. (This timing can vary considerably depending on how thinly the batter is spread and how long it is cooked in the saucepan.)

A feast is made for laughter...

—THE BOOK OF ECCLESIASTES

Company
Chicken Tostadas

A real special occasion treat! We call them "Mexican Mountains"
and have served them to over 50 football players and cheerleaders.

Ingredients

>   refried beans
>   guacamole
>   sour cream and plain yogurt
>   chicken, cooked and shredded
>   cheddar cheese, grated
>   raw vegetables
>   olives
>   corn tortillas

Preparation

Before heating and assembling the tortillas, have all the ingredients prepared in desired amounts. Bake corn tortillas, 1 per serving. Place directly on oven rack, single layer, in a 350 degree oven for 10 to 12 minutes. Arrange over each crispy tortilla for individual servings in the following order:

> ⅓ to ½ cup refried beans
> 1   cup shredded lettuce, mixed dark leafy and iceberg
> 2   tablespoons to ¼ cup grated cheddar cheese
> ¼ to ½ cup shredded cooked chicken
> ¼ to ½ cup guacamole
> 1 to 2 tablespoons yogurt/sour cream blend (half and half)
> 5   cherry tomatoes or ½ tomato cut in wedges
> 3 to 6 whole ripe olives
>   sprigs of fresh parsley

The Perfect Pantry

Whether your pantry is a separate room or a couple of shelves in your cupboards, it's an essential element in organizing meals and saving money. I recommend that a pantry contain a supply of basic staple foods, including starches, sweets, condiments, and canned or bottled items.

Starches
flour
pasta
cornmeal
white and/or brown rice
boxed cereal
oatmeal
a variety of potatoes

Sweet-based Staples
honey
maple syrup
brown and white sugar
jams and jellies
apple juice

Condiments
ketchup
brown and/or yellow mustard
vinegar
oil
pickles
olives
capers
salsa
Worcestershire sauce
canned tuna or any other canned fish or meat

Dried or Canned Fruits and Vegetables
green beans
tomatoes
fruit cocktail
applesauce
raisins
prunes
variety of soups

Making the Most of Your Pantry

Here are a few helpful hints for making the most of your pantry:

- When stocking your pantry, organize your staples and canned goods in categories such as canned fruit, canned vegetables, meats, juices, cereals, etc.

- Keep an inventory of your pantry. Plan your menus using this list and shop only once a week, replenishing staples as necessary. Restock *before* you run out to avoid those "emergency" trips to the grocery store when unexpected company arrives.

- Place a colored dot on items you've purchased for a future recipe to warn your husband and children that these are not to be used for snacks.

- Investigate using a food service. It allows you to save time and money by shopping on the phone and ordering staples for six months at a time. This way your weekly shopping is limited to perishables, and often you can zip through the express line at the checkout counter.

Calico Beans

*Our office manager used to bring a pot of these
calico beans to our office for a yummy lunch on a cold, wintry day.*

Ingredients

1   pound ground beef or ground turkey
1   pound bacon, cooked and drained (cut into 1 inch
        pieces)
1   medium onion, chopped
1   green pepper, chopped
½   cup brown sugar
½   cup ketchup
1   16-ounce can kidney beans
1   16-ounce can lima beans
1   15-ounce can B&M baked beans
1   15-ounce can garbanzo beans
1   small can corn (optional)

Preparation

Brown meats, drain well, and mix together with all other ingredients except corn. Add corn before serving for additional color. Cook as a thick soup over medium/low heat. Also may be baked in a roaster covered with dollops of corn bread dough (bake according to corn bread directions).

This recipe is great in a Crock-Pot, cooked all day on low… presto—dinner's ready! This makes a very thick full-bodied chili-type soup.

Baby Back Ribs or Chicken

*A dear family friend comes to our home and makes
this recipe for us as a special treat. We all eat, eat, and eat.*

Ingredients

ribs or chicken (depending on number of guests)
Lawry's 17 Seasonings
pepper
garlic salt

1   16-ounce bottle Newman's Own Italian Dressing
1   16-ounce bottle Knott's Honey Mustard Dressing
1   28-ounce bottle Bullseye Original BBQ Sauce
1   small bottle Kikoman Teriyaki Baste and Glaze

Preparation

Trim excess fat or skin from ribs, rinse under warm water.
Sprinkle both sides with Lawry's 17 Seasonings, pepper, and
garlic salt. Stir together Newman's Own Italian Dressing and
Knott's Honey Mustard Dressing. Coat both sides of meat and
marinate at least 2 hours. I like to let it sit in the refrigerator
overnight. Simmer on stove about 1 hour on low heat. The meat
will start to pull away from the bone. Mix together Bullseye Original BBQ Sauce and Kikoman Teriyaki Baste and Glaze. Put
meat on grill. Turn meat until light brown on both sides. Coat 1
side with BBQ mix. Let cook about 2 minutes. Turn and coat.
Repeat this step until meat appears thick and gooey.

Lemon Herb Chicken

SERVES 4

Ingredients

1 ½   pounds chicken breasts, skinned and boneless

For marinade combine in a jar, cover tightly, and shake well:
>   juice of 2 lemons (about ½ cup)
¼   teaspoon garlic powder
¼   teaspoon thyme leaves
¼   teaspoon marjoram leaves
¼   teaspoon salt
⅛   teaspoon rosemary leaves, crushed
>   paprika (optional)

Preparation

Pour marinade into shallow glass baking dish or pie plate. Arrange chicken in single layer in marinade. Cover and marinate in refrigerator at least 1 hour or in microwave oven on low for 6 minutes, turning pieces over halfway through. Bake uncovered at 350 degrees for 1 hour, basting with marinade every 20 minutes. If top of chicken reaches desired brownness before chicken is done, turn pieces over, or cover with foil to complete baking. Garnish with paprika to serve.

Serve with wild rice, broccoli, orange slices.

Emilie's
Noodle Bake

A really simple casserole to make. Make a very quick
meal by adding tossed salad and French bread.

Ingredients

8	ounce-package flat spinach noodles
4	quarts boiling water
¼	teaspoon salt
1	teaspoon oil
¼	teaspoon pepper
1	pound ground turkey
2	cups pasta or spaghetti sauce
1	pint (2 cups) cottage cheese

Preparation

To cook pasta, add noodles, salt, and oil to boiling water and cook until barely tender 7 to 10 minutes; drain. Brown the turkey and combine with remaining ingredients. Stir in cooked noodles and place in casserole. Heat covered in oven at 350 degrees for about 30 minutes. Serve immediately.

Texas Meat Loaf

This recipe is from Great Grandma Gertie's kitchen. Born in Texas in 1914, she made it for our family and served it with baked potatoes and fresh green beans.

Ingredients

1 ½	pounds lean ground beef (or ¾ pound beef and ¾ pound turkey)
¼	pound Jimmy Dean Hot Sausage
3	cloves garlic, chopped
1	medium onion, chopped
1	green pepper, chopped
1	tablespoon A-1 sauce
¾	cup oatmeal
2	eggs, beaten
3	slices bread, soaked in milk (squeeze out milk)
1	12-ounce bottle Heinz Chili Sauce (I use about 10 ounces of it.)
	salt and pepper to taste

Preparation

In a large bowl, mix all ingredients well with hands. Form in two loaves and put in a 13" x 9" dish and bake at 350 degrees for about 1 ½ hours. Cool 15 minutes before slicing. I always put the rest of the chili sauce on top to make it look pretty.

Perfect Peeling

Four quick and easy ways to peel:

- ❧ Cut off the bottom of an onion, then the top. Cut a slash in the side and remove the first outer peel, including the skin.

- ❧ Turn a fork-held tomato over a gas burner until the skin begins to darken and blister. It will peel right off.

- ❧ Place tomatoes in boiling water and remove pan from heat. Let sit for one minute. Remove the tomatoes from the pan, plunge them into cold water, and strip off the skins.

- ❧ With the palm of your hand, crush the entire head of garlic so that the cloves fall apart. Select one clove and place the flat side of a large knife over it; hit the knife gently with your hand. The clove skin will come off immediately. To get the smell of garlic off your hands, rub them in used coffee grounds or lemon juice.

❧

It's good food, not fine words, that will keep me alive.

—WILSON MIZNER

Judy Brixey's
Beef Casserole
SERVES 6-10

Better known as "Train Wreck" by our kids,
this recipe can usually be
made from whatever is on hand
in the fridge or the pantry.

Ingredients
1   pound lean ground beef (or turkey) browned with
          1 chopped onion and 2 to 3 cloves minced garlic.
     Pour off any excess fat.

Pasta
Any type of pasta or rice that when cooked makes about 3 cups.

Liquid
Either one 28-ounce can chopped tomatoes including juice
or 3 to 4 chopped fresh tomatoes plus one 15-ounce can tomato
sauce or spaghetti sauce.

Crunch
1   cup chopped celery, microwaved for 4 minutes
2   cups cooked corn

Optional
1   cup sour cream
1   cup cheese, grated (maybe a combination of cheddar,
          Jack or Parmesan)
     black olives, chopped or sliced
     fresh basil leaves, torn
     parsley, chopped

Season to taste:
> salt, regular or seasoned
> pepper
> hot sauce to jazz it up

You may add oregano or herbs de provence, or 1 to 2 table-spoons Worcestershire sauce. As you can see, there are endless variations and you can double the amounts indefinitely.

Preparation
Bake covered in the oven for 40 minutes at 325-350 degrees, or you can simmer on low on the stove in a heavy bottomed pan with lid.

Broiled
Game Hens with Apple-Thyme Glaze
SERVES 2

Ingredients
> 3   teaspoons olive oil
> 1   tablespoon minced onion
> 2   tablespoons apple jelly
> 1   teaspoon chopped thyme or ½ teaspoon dried, crumbled
> 2   teaspoons cider vinegar
> 1   large Cornish game hen (about 1 ½ pounds), cut in half, backbone discarded
>   salt and pepper
>   apple slices (optional)
>   fresh thyme sprigs (optional)

Preparation

Preheat broiler. Heat 2 teaspoons oil in small heavy saucepan over low heat. Add onion and sauté until translucent, about 2 minutes. Add apple jelly and chopped thyme and stir until jelly melts. Mix in vinegar. Set glaze aside.

Rub hen halves with remaining teaspoon oil. Season with salt and pepper. Place hen halves skin side down in broiler pan. Broil about 5 inches from heat source until brown and crisp, 10 minutes. Brush glaze over. Turn hen halves over. Broil skin side up until just cooked through and juices from thigh run clear when pierced, 5 minutes. Brush skin with glaze and broil just until glaze begins to color; about 1 minute. Broil 15 minutes per pound; continue glazing and rotating.

Arrange hen halves on plates. Garnish with apple slices and thyme.

Accompany with baked winter squash and buttered, steamed cauliflower.

℃

Spice a dish with love and
it pleases every palate.
—PLAUTUS

Vegetable
Smothered Chicken

SERVES 4

Ingredients

3 pounds chicken, skinned and cut up
¾ cup sherry or white wine
   arrowroot or flour
3 tablespoons butter or olive oil
1 onion, chopped
4 carrots, cut in thirds crosswise
½ pound fresh mushrooms, sliced
4 green onions, sliced
¼ teaspoon red pepper
½ teaspoon garlic powder
1 teaspoon vegetable salt

Preparation

Marinate chicken in white wine at least 2 hours. Remove chicken and blot with paper towels, but reserve the marinade. Dredge chicken in arrowroot or flour; brown lightly in butter or oil and remove from pan. Add vegetables and seasonings, put lid on and continue cooking until onion browns lightly. Return chicken to pan, add wine and simmer, covered, for 35 minutes or until chicken becomes tender.

Serve with orange muffins, rice, and a green vegetable.

Italian Zucchini Frittata

SERVES 4

This is a good way to use zucchini in an omelet, and it's a delicious supper.

Ingredients

4	cups zucchini (about 1 ½ pounds), unpeeled and grated
2	tablespoons onion, chopped
½	teaspoon garlic, chopped
4	eggs
2	tablespoons skim milk
½	teaspoon dried oregano
½	teaspoon dried basil
¼	teaspoon pepper
½	teaspoon salt (optional)
2	tablespoons Parmesan cheese

Preparation

Spray a 10-inch skillet with a non-stick coating. Sauté first three ingredients until zucchini is tender, pouring off any liquid. Meanwhile, mix eggs, milk, and seasonings (except cheese). Add to the zucchini mixture and cook until the eggs begin to set. Top with Parmesan cheese. Broil just until top is golden.

Serve with hot tortillas and butter.

Chicken Fajitas

Serves 4

Ingredients

- 3 tablespoons lime juice
- ½ teaspoon ground coriander
- ½ teaspoon chili powder
- 1 pound boneless, skinless chicken breasts, cut into 1 inch strips
- 1 green pepper, sliced
- 1 onion, sliced
- 8 flour tortillas (6 inch size)

   salsa (optional)

Preparation

Mix lime juice with coriander and chili powder and pour over chicken. Set aside. Meanwhile, slice vegetables. Add to chicken and mix well. Spray pan with non-stick coating and stir-fry chicken and vegetables until done. Warm tortillas in microwave about 50 seconds on high or in non-stick skillet. Fill each tortilla with chicken mixture and serve with salsa. This meal is great with black beans.

Chicken and Rice, the Mexican Way

SERVES 8

Ingredients

1	medium onion, chopped
1	green pepper, chopped
1	teaspoon garlic, minced
1	16-ounce can canned tomatoes
1	4-ounce can chopped chiles
1	14 ½-ounce can chicken broth, fat removed
1 ¾	cups quick cooking brown rice
6	drops Tabasco sauce
2	pounds boneless, skinless chicken breasts
¼	cup cheddar cheese, grated

Preparation

Preheat oven to 350 degrees. Sauté onion and pepper in a skillet that has been sprayed with non-stick coating. Add next six ingredients. Mix well and bring to a boil. Remove from heat and spoon into a 9" x 13" baking pan that has been sprayed with non-stick coating. Arrange chicken on top of rice mixture. Bake, covered, for 35 minutes or until rice is done. Sprinkle cheese over chicken, let stand 5 minutes or until cheese is melted.

Making the Most of Leftovers

🌿 Have some cooked meat left over, but not enough for an entire meal? Chop it up small, add a small amount of mayonnaise, bell pepper, celery, etc., and you have a great salad spread for sandwiches.

🌿 Spread almost-stale bread with butter or margarine and sprinkle with grated cheese. Toast and top with a poached egg.

🌿 When I have a few crumbs left in a bag of potato chips or box of crackers, I save them. After I lightly coat them with butter and toast them in the oven until brown, they make a tasty topping for casseroles or baked vegetables.

🌿 For the two of us I bake six large potatoes. We eat them baked the first night. The second serving is sliced and fried in a bit of butter. The last two potatoes are cubed and served in a cream sauce with some cheese.

🌿 Don't throw out the last cup of chili, beans, stew, or casserole—put it in a Tupperware container. At the end of the month, dump them all in a pot. Presto—a great surprise dish!

🌿 Make homemade TV dinners from leftovers. Label them as follows: "Goulash/Date/Micro: High—one minute/Salad and Bread." By suggesting the cooking time and menu complement, you'll find that the leftovers are eaten, meals are rarely skipped, and money is saved!

🌿 When serving leftover meat or fish, don't just reheat it. Prepare it in a different form. For example, grind it and shape it into patties, dice it for casseroles, or slice it thin and add to stir-fry dishes or to a white sauce.

🌿 Turn your no-longer-fresh bread and crackers into crumbs for use in stuffings, casseroles, and meat loaf. Just put them in the blender, turn it on, and count to three. Then put the crumbs in a plastic bag for storage.

🌿 Leftover orange, lemon, or lime rinds are great garbage disposal deodorizers.

Sweet and Sour Chicken

SERVES 5

Serve this recipe over rice or noodles.

Ingredients

1	8-ounce can unsweetened pineapple chunks, packed in juice
1	pound boneless, skinless chicken breasts
1	cup chicken broth (low-fat if you like)
¼	cup vinegar
¼	cup brown sugar
2	teaspoons soy sauce
½	teaspoon garlic, chopped
1	cup celery, sliced
1	small onion, quartered
1	green pepper, sliced
3	tablespoons cornstarch
¼	cup water

Preparation

Drain pineapple, reserving the juice. Cut chicken into bite-size pieces and place in a saucepan. Add reserved juice, broth, vinegar, brown sugar, soy sauce, and garlic. Cover and simmer over low heat for 15 minutes. Add vegetables and pineapple. Cook 10 minutes, stirring occasionally. Combine cornstarch and water. Gradually stir into hot mixture. Continue to cook until thickened, stirring constantly. Serve with quick-cooking brown rice.

Saucy
Spaghetti Squash

SERVES 6

A delightfully different and meatless way to serve spaghetti.

Ingredients

2   tablespoons olive oil
1   onion, chopped
2   cloves garlic, minced
1   medium carrot, chopped small
1   green pepper, chopped
1   cup fresh mushrooms, sliced, or 4-ounce can sliced
      mushrooms
1   quart of spaghetti sauce (Ragu Homestyle is a good one)
1   medium spaghetti squash (4 pounds)

Preparation

To prepare sauce, sauté vegetables in oil, adding green pepper and mushrooms when onion and carrot are just tender. Add sauce and simmer 30 minutes to blend flavors. Meanwhile, to cook spaghetti squash, halve squash, remove seeds. Place half the squash cut side up in shallow dish, add ¼ cup water, cover lightly with plastic wrap, and microwave for 7 to 8 minutes; let stand 5 minutes. Repeat with second half (or you may boil whole, covered with water 20 to 30 minutes; or bake at 400 degrees about 1 hour, then halve and remove seeds).

Run a fork around sides of cooked squash and pull out the spaghetti strings, place into a large mixing bowl.

Serve sauce over spaghetti squash, top with Parmesan cheese, if desired. It may be baked for 15 minutes at 350 degrees, if desired.

A Light
Italian Pasta Deluxe

SERVES 6-8

Some say this is a favorite recipe that actor James Garner cooks.

Ingredients

olive oil
1   garlic clove, chopped
1   green pepper, chopped
1   small onion, chopped
½   pound ground sirloin or ground turkey
1   14 ½-ounce can whole tomatoes, drained
1   15-ounce can or 1 cup frozen corn
½   a 10 ¾-ounce can tomato soup
½   cup cheddar cheese, grated
½   teaspoon chili powder
¼   teaspoon cayenne pepper
salt and pepper to taste
¾   pound pasta (whatever kind you have on hand)

Preparation

In hot oil, sauté garlic, green pepper, and onion until thoroughly cooked. Add meat, cook until browned. Add the tomatoes, corn, and tomato soup; mix well. Add grated cheese and stir until melted. Stir in chili powder, cayenne pepper, salt, and pepper to taste. Remove from heat and set aside.

Cook pasta according to package directions, drain. Add sauce, mix thoroughly, and place into a 2 quart casserole. Preheat the oven to 325 degrees. Bake uncovered, just until hot.

Eat-Every-Week
Chicken Veggie Bake

SERVES 4

This is a real favorite, especially with our grandchildren.

Ingredients

1	3 to 4 pound chicken
3	tablespoons vegetable oil, divided
	salt and pepper to taste
2	large onions, chopped
½	cup chicken broth or water
5	large potatoes, cubed
1	large green pepper, seeded and diced
5	large carrots, sliced
4	stalks celery, sliced

Preparation

Preheat the oven to 425 degrees.

Brush chicken with 1 tablespoon oil and sprinkle with a little salt and pepper. Place in a roasting pan, brown chicken for 20 minutes. Sauté the onions in remaining oil until nicely browned, stir in chicken broth or water. Arrange potatoes, green pepper, carrots, and celery around the chicken and pour browned onions over all. Sprinkle with a little pepper.

Cover and bake for 1 ½ hours at 350 degrees.

The browned onions enhance the flavor of the chicken and other vegetables. This is a great buffet dish, along with sweet pickles, fresh green salad, hot rolls, and pie.

Family Roasted Chicken

SERVES 4

*Our daughter, Jenny, wins great compliments
from her family with this meal.*

Ingredients

- 1   whole chicken (4 to 4 ½ pounds)
       salt and freshly ground black pepper
- 1   cup water
- ¼   cup extra-virgin olive oil
- ¼   cup unsalted butter, at room temperature

You can add red potatoes, carrots, and celery if you like, right at the start, and have a meal-in-one!

Preparation

Preheat the oven to 475 degrees.

Place the chicken in a shallow baking dish. Sprinkle the chicken, inside and out, with salt and pepper. Drizzle with the olive oil and dot with butter. Place in the upper half of the oven and cook for 45 minutes, basting every 7 minutes. Be sure to move the chicken around a bit to ensure that it is not sticking to the dish.

After 45 minutes, turn off the oven, leave the chicken in the oven for 10 minutes longer and then remove. Let rest for 10 minutes.

Move the chicken to a platter; discard the fat in the baking dish. Add the water to the baking dish and whisk well, scraping up all of the brown bits on the bottom of the dish. Remove the sauce to a small saucepan. Bring the sauce to a boil and cook for 3 minutes. Season with salt and pepper to taste.

Carve the chicken, adding any carving juices to the sauce. Serve immediately and pour the sauce in a gravy boat.

Lamb Stew

SERVES 4

Growing up in a Jewish home,
I ate a lot of lamb—I still love lamb of all kinds.

Ingredients

4	tablespoons olive oil
1	medium onion, chopped
2	cloves garlic, minced
1	pound lamb shoulder cut into 1 inch cubes
3	cups chicken broth
2	carrots, sliced
1	stalk celery, chopped
½	cup dry sherry
¼	teaspoon parsley, chopped
½	green onion, chopped
	salt and pepper

Preparation

In a large pot, heat 2 tablespoons olive oil; sauté onion and garlic until translucent. Add the lamb shoulder and another 2 tablespoons olive oil. Sauté lamb until lightly browned. Add the chicken broth, carrots, celery, dry sherry, parsley, and green onion.

Bring to boil, reduce heat, and simmer until lamb is tender, about 1 hour, skimming any foam from surface. Season to taste with salt and pepper.

Broccoli-Cheese Casserole

This dish from Sheri Torelli goes great with turkey, chicken, or just about any kind of meat.

Ingredients
- ⅓ cup butter, melted (⅔ stick)
- ½ cup onion, chopped
- 1 14-ounce bag frozen broccoli (thaw to room temperature)
- 1 can cream of chicken soup
- 1 small jar of Cheez Whiz (8 ounce)
- 1 cup Minute Rice (uncooked)

Preparation
Sauté onions in butter; add all other ingredients. Bake in a buttered 2 quart casserole dish for 30 to 40 minutes at 350 degrees. (You may microwave for 10 to 15 minutes in a microwave dish.) This recipe is very easy to double, triple, or whatever.

℀

The cheerful heart has a continual feast.
—THE BOOK OF PROVERBS

Clever Tricks with Fruits
and Vegetables

❦ Never store carrots with apples. Apples release a gas that gives carrots a bitter taste.

❦ Don't throw away a soup or stew that has turned out too salty. Instead, add a cut raw potato, and discard the potato slices when they are cooked. The potato will absorb most of the salt.

❦ When cooking vegetables in water, leave them whole. They'll retain more vitamins and minerals, and they're much easier to chop or slice after they're cooked.

❦ Slice raw tomatoes vertically so the inner pulp holds its shape for salads.

❦ Sautéed diced vegetables make a delicious low-calorie topping for pasta, baked potatoes, or rice.

❦ To get more juice out of a lemon, place it in your microwave on "high" for 30 seconds. Squeeze the lemon, and you will get twice as much juice—and the vitamins won't be lost.

❦ A great way to clean fresh mushrooms is to add three to four tablespoons of flour to a medium-size bowl of cold water. Wash the mushrooms in the water. The dirt adheres to the flour particles almost like magic. The mushrooms come out very clean.

❦ Never slice your onion to make soup. Just peel and put the whole onion in to make a sweeter pot.

Barbecue
Chicken Pizza

My friend Marita Littauer Noon concocted this recipe at the request of her husband, Chuck. It's become a favorite of theirs.

Ingredients

1   Boboli pizza crust, original
3   tablespoons olive oil (I use basil-flavored olive oil)
     barbecue sauce
1   red onion cut into 8 wedges, separated
1   red pepper, cut into ⅛ inch long strips
1   green pepper, cut into ⅛ inch long strips
2 to 3 boneless chicken breasts
1   cup cheddar cheese, grated
1   cup Monterey Jack cheese, grated
½   cup Parmesan cheese, freshly grated
1   4-ounce can olives, sliced

Preparation

Prepare barbecue, preheat oven to 400 degrees.

Place pizza crust on cookie sheet. Lightly brush crust with oil. Heavily brush with barbecue sauce. Set aside.

Brush chicken breasts with barbecue sauce. Grill for approximately 4 minutes per side or until cooked through.

Meanwhile, heat 1 tablespoon of olive oil in a large skillet over medium/high heat. Add onion and peppers and sauté until soft and slightly browned, about 8 minutes.

Cut chicken crosswise into rough strips.

To assemble the pizza, sprinkle the cooked vegetables over crust. Evenly distribute the chicken pieces. Top with cheeses, then olives. Place in oven for 10 minutes, then slice and serve.

Southwestern Chicken Pasta

SERVES 4

Another wonderful recipe from my friend Marita.

Ingredients

 3 tablespoons butter
 2 large red bell peppers, cut into ¼ inch strips
 3 garlic cloves, minced
 ¾ teaspoon cayenne pepper
 3 to 4 chicken breasts, boneless
    salt and pepper
 12 ounces penne pasta
 1 cup frozen peas
 1 cup whipping cream
 ¾ cup chicken broth
 ¾ cup Parmesan cheese, freshly grated
 ¾ cup Monterey Jack cheese, grated
 1 tablespoon fresh basil, chopped

Preparation

Melt butter in large heavy skillet over medium heat. Add bell peppers, garlic, and cayenne; stir to blend. Cover skillet; cook until peppers are tender, stirring occasionally, about 8 minutes.

Meanwhile, sprinkle chicken breasts with salt and pepper and grill until cooked through, about 4 minutes per side. Diagonally slice chicken and set aside.

Using a large pot, cook pasta according to package directions. Add peas during the last 5 minutes of cooking time. Drain. Return peas and pasta to pot.

Uncover skillet, add cream and broth and simmer until liquid is slightly thickened, about 5 minutes. Stir in ½ cup of Parmesan cheese, Monterey Jack cheese, and basil. Remove from heat.

Gently blend bell pepper/sauce mixture and pasta. Place pasta on individual plates and top with sliced chicken and remaining Parmesan.

℮

At feasts, remember that you are entertaining two guests,
body and soul. What you give to the body, you presently lose;
what you give to the soul, you keep forever.

—EPICTETUS

Ground Turkey and Angel Hair Pasta with Tomato Cream Sauce

SERVES 4

This is an extremely easy entrée from Marita, suitable for a company dinner.

Ingredients

1	teaspoon olive oil
1 ½	pounds ground turkey
1	cup green onions, sliced
2	14 ½-ounce cans diced peeled tomatoes
1	cup whipping cream
½	cup white wine
1	tablespoon tomato paste
1	16-ounce package angel hair pasta
	Parmesan cheese, freshly grated

Preparation

Heat oil in a large skillet over medium heat. Add the turkey and green onions, sauté until cooked through about 10 minutes. Stir frequently throughout cooking to break up the ground turkey. Add tomatoes with their liquid, cream, wine, and tomato paste. Simmer until sauce thickens, about 10 minutes.

Meanwhile, cook pasta according to package directions.

When sauce is ready, add the cooked pasta and toss until blended. Season to taste with salt and pepper. Place on individual plates, sprinkle with Parmesan cheese, and serve.

Skinny Chicken
a la Judy

My friend Judy Goyette has created a recipe
that is virtually fat free.

Ingredients

    6 to 8 boneless, skinless chicken breasts
       celery salt
       paprika
       tarragon with lemon slices or chopped, dried garlic
  1   chicken bouillon cube, disolved in 1 cup water
  2   tablespoons onion flakes
  4   tablespoons white wine

Preparation

Preheat oven to 350 degrees. Rinse chicken breasts, and lightly salt both sides with celery salt while putting into large roasting pan. Paprika the tops (they will not brown). Sprinkle either tarragon or chopped garlic over the tops (add one slice of lemon to each breast when using tarragon).

For sauce, microwave bouillon and onion flakes for at least one minute before adding the white wine. Pour over chicken breasts and cover pan tightly. Bake for 25 minutes; uncover and continue baking for another 25 minutes. Serve immediately or cool and freeze.

Serve with rice pilaf, salad, and a veggie.

Chicken Fling

SERVES 4

My friend Sheri Torelli got this recipe from her dear friend, Wilma Glidewell. It is very low in fat and delicious!

Ingredients

1   whole chicken cut up (5 to 6 pieces) or 4 to 5 boneless, skinless chicken breasts

1   package Lipton Onion Soup Mix

1   10-ounce jar orange marmalade

Preparation

Use a 9" x 13" glass pan. Place chicken in the pan. Sprinkle onion soup mix over the chicken. Spread orange marmalade on top of the chicken and soup mix. Cover with aluminum foil and bake at 350 degrees for approximately 35 minutes.

ℰ

But come along, come into the kitchen.
There's a first-rate fire there,
and supper and everything.

—KENNETH GRAHAME
The Wind in the Willows

"The Stuff"

*This buffet type meal-in-one from Janie Gaskins is
a crowd pleaser! It will serve large groups very easily.*

Ingredients

> Minute Rice (quantity depends on how many people you
> are going to serve)
> canned chili (no beans)
> Fritos corn chips (crushed)
> cheese, grated (cheddar, Jack, mozzarella)
> sliced or chopped olives (drain excess juice)
> peanuts, chopped
> coconut, shredded
> avocado, cut up in small chunks
> tomatoes, chopped
> lettuce, shredded
> chopped green chiles
> jalapeños
> salsa
> sour cream

Preparation

Make a large pan each of Minute Rice (per directions) and
chili. All other ingredients are to be placed in separate bowls.
Start with rice, add some chili, and then use your creativity and
personal taste from there. Top off your plate with sour cream. You
may add or delete ingredients depending on your preferences.
Serve with warm flour tortillas and enjoy!

Donna Otto's
Pasta Gravy

Ingredients

½   onion, chopped
1   clove garlic, chopped
3   tablespoons olive oil
2   6-ounce cans tomato paste
2   cups peeled tomatoes mashed and blended in blender,
       or 1 16-ounce can tomatoes
6   cups water
1   teaspoon oregano
1   teaspoon basil
½   teaspoon seeds fennel
1   tablespoon salt

Preparation

Brown onion and garlic in olive oil. Add tomato paste. Stir for 3 to 5 minutes over medium heat. Add peeled tomatoes and water. Stir well. Add oregano, basil, fennel, and salt. Simmer on low for 3 hours, stir well and often.

So simple it takes about 7 minutes to put together! I always double the recipe.

This gravy (Italians call it gravy because they put it on everything) will freeze wonderfully, and it does go over anything: pastas, vegetables, meat, and lasagna dishes.

Menu

Loaf of sour dough bread, sliced and brushed with melted garlic butter. Brush each slice and across the top, wrap in foil keeping the top open so the bread is soft in the center...crunchy on top.

Tossed salad with wine vinegar and olive oil dressing
Pasta, any kind. Our favorites are capelini and mostaccoli.
Gravy (see previous page)
Fresh grated Romano cheese

Dessert

One 3-ounce package strawberry Jell-O, jelled; 2 cups of vanilla ice cream, and fresh strawberries. Put ice cream and Jell-O in mixing bowl and beat at medium speed until blended. Pour into individual dessert dishes...top with fresh berries.

The entire meal is done in advance...so you can be available to your family and friends.

*Small cheer and great welcome
make a merry feast.*

—SHAKESPEARE

Five Tips That Make a Difference

❦ If you take out all ingredients at the beginning of a cooking project and put them away as used, the cleanup is easier and there's no doubt whether or not you have used an ingredient.

❦ Favorite recipes that you use often, whether cut from magazines or written on recipe cards, can be taped to the inside of your kitchen cabinet doors. When you're ready to cook, there's no need to rummage through clippings in envelopes or boxes. Just open your cabinet door!

❦ When shopping, don't deviate from your grocery list unless you find unadvertised sales, such as overripe fruit and day-old bakery items.

❦ For those times you can't cook, prepare a small book titled "Mom's (or Dad's) Helpful Hints," in which you record easy-to-prepare recipes. Carefully note each step for every recipe and include some special cooking tips. Your family will really appreciate it.

❦ Don't forget to use your microwave, even when making a conventional recipe. Let it melt butter and chocolate, soften cheese toast nuts, cook bacon, and thaw frozen vegetables.

❦

When a man's stomach is full it makes no difference
whether he is rich or poor.

—EURIPIDES

Index of Recipes

For more information regarding speaking engagements
and additional material, please send a self-addressed
envelope to:

More Hours in My Day
2150 Whitestone Dr.
Riverside, CA 92506

Or you can visit us on the Internet at:
www.emiliebarnes.com
or
emilie@emiliebarnes.com